iCommunism

Capitalism promised us shiny things
but only communism can deliver them
in a different, more liberating,
universal and sustainable form

iCommunism

Capitalism promised us shiny things
but only communism can deliver them
in a different, more liberating,
universal and sustainable form

Colin Cremin

Winchester, UK
Washington, USA

First published by Zero Books, 2012
Zero Books is an imprint of John Hunt Publishing Ltd., Laurel House, Station Approach,
Alresford, Hants, SO24 9JH, UK
office1@jhpbooks.net
www.johnhuntpublishing.com
www.zero-books.net

For distributor details and how to order please visit the 'Ordering' section on our website.

ISBN: 978 1 78099 229 7

A CIP catalogue record for this book is available from the British Library.

Design: Stuart Davies

Printed in the USA by Edwards Brothers Malloy

We operate a distinctive and ethical publishing philosophy in all
areas of our business, from our global network of authors to
production and worldwide distribution.

CONTENTS

Acknowledgements

First of all I would like to thank the people at Zero for making this possible, including Trevor Greenfield, Stuart Davies and Tariq Goddard who was so quick and helpful in responding to questions. My gratitude to Anaise Irvine for reviewing the draft prior to submission and Siobhan McKeown for reviewing the submitted draft, both provided valuable comments without any hassle or delay. I would like to thank the Faculty of Arts at Auckland for providing a grant in support of this and other projects. This includes funding 3 excellent research assistants: Jai Bentley-Payne, Shanti Daellenbach and Aria Jones. I would also like to express a general indebtedness to all critical utopians and students of the courses I teach who, by thought, dialogue and action, have been an inspiration. I thank friends and colleagues in the Department of Sociology – Steve Matthewman and David Mayeda in particular - for their contributions in creating a great working environment and their intellectual and emotional support during the period that I wrote the book. And, finally, thank you to Akiko Horita who adds the 'i' to my world.

0.0 Introduction

Even Marxists like to shop

I like the light that reflects on the calm surface of the River Tyne, the same light that reflects on the surface of my new iPad. I am drawn to streets bathed in neon, streets that by day are packed with the books, CDs, DVDs, and those fancy saucepans (the ones in bright colours with heavy bases) that I desire. A junkie to commerce, I was born watching adverts, and despite what I know about all the side effects of production - the exploited labour, waste and environmental degradation – I still consume and consume in excess of my needs. Probably compensating for the anxieties advertisers have manipulated and the alienation at the core of my being, the bind I am in is near universal – at least in the West. In short, I am duped by capital into wanting things I do not need, things that in various ways I have come to depend on even though the costs of consuming them are prohibitive beyond measure. Herbert Marcuse, a trenchant critic of consumerism writing in a more distant age of rising affluence, speaks to me and surely many of us when he wrote: 'the so-called consumer economy and the politics of corporate capitalism have created a second nature of man which ties him libidinally and aggressively to the commodity form.'[1] Commerce has turned us into half-lives, shells of a fuller self, and in our identities we have become, if the clichéd phrase 'I shop therefore I am' has any truth to it, mirrors of the things desired and consumed. Objects that fill our homes and imaginations fit our identities like gloves because our natures are so bound and stunted by relations of exchange. The so-called consumer society has not liberated the senses so much as retarded them. Austerity threatens their suffocation.

iCommunism is a book about consumption and desire, about the degradations of consumerism, the highs and lows, from affluence through to austerity. It is a book about the liberation of the senses, the freeing of the pleasure principle or *Eros* from the institutions of the reality principle: a reality of corruption, brutality, venality, exploitation and soon ecological catastrophe. It is a book on the dirty water in which consumers bathe with a title that steals the lustre from Phones, Pads and Pods, the fetishised lower case i, proposing to bring it under common ownership to liberate the senses from the commodity form and nature from its infernal logic.

All roads lead to austerity

Whereas consumption is a practice common to cave- and condo-dwellers, consumerism turns consumption into a religion that shapes how an entire people desire, think and socialise. The consumer has no class, gender or ethnicity, no place, depth or distinction. The word *consumer*, said Raymond Williams, 'is now habitually used by people to whom it ought, logically, to be repugnant.'[2] Not only does the word debase us, it reframes concerns about the world as questions of individual morality.

Consumers have become the scourge of society. It is our crass individualism, selfishness, and greed that so corrodes public life and has contributed to the depletion of planetary resources, the rise of sweatshops in India, and skyrocketing food prices in Africa. And now, by 'binging on easy credit', we are also to blame for the economic crisis. Six months after the collapse of Lehman Brother's investment bank, a Washington Post-ABC news poll reported that 7 in 10 Americans held consumers responsible for the economic crisis for having overextended themselves.[3] Barack Obama echoed the sentiment two months later:

One of the causes of this economic crisis was that too many people were living beyond their means with mortgages they couldn't afford, buying things they couldn't pay for, maxing out on credit cards that they couldn't pay down... We've

2

contributed to our own problems. We've got to change how we operate. But these practices, they've only grown worse in the midst of this recession, when hardworking Americans can afford them least.[4]

Our hands had been caught in the till, and so it was time to take the punishment. Fast-forward to Greece in 2010. A commentator for the *Guardian* wrote in response to the popular mobilisations against the IMF bailouts that 'it's time to take the pain... we did this to ourselves and there's no choice but to put on a brave face and forge a "New Greece".' March 2011 saw the first national demonstration against public sector cutbacks in Britain. 57% of respondents to a survey commissioned by the *Guardian* thought the cutbacks were necessary.[5] This crisis is a case in which, as Deleuze and Guattari put it, 'desire is shamed, stupefied... it is easily persuaded to deny "itself" in the name of more important interests of civilisation'.[6] The pill of austerity might be bitter, but it is one that people seem all too ready to swallow, if not for economic reasons then at least for ecological ones.

Austerity is our past, the co-present and a possible future. It permeates through all class-based societies: primitive and advanced, capitalist, former communist, and prospective eco-rational. The liberation of the senses that Marcuse advocated has no chance, especially when the alternatives to capitalism appear just as (if not more) repressive than capitalism itself. The imagination lingers on images of bread queues and weatherworn faces from a 'really existing' socialist past; an alternative that no sensuous being would aspire to. In the 21st Century there are only the faintest of echoes of utopia when, on Saturdays in town, more dogmatic socialists compete with cranks for the attention of passing shoppers. The imagination suffers from these assaults. It is beaten into submission by the tableau of colourful products in shop window displays. And if cynicism has blocked one utopia, the checkout has blocked another. Yet there is an alternative to what Mark Fisher calls 'capitalist realism' – the presupposition that the market is the only game in town – and that alternative does not have to be mapped to austerity, whether justified on economic or ecological grounds. The alternative can be something altogether shinier and joyful.

Critics of consumerism have hitherto only wanted us to tighten our belts in various ways; the point is to burn them
Critiques of the consumer society make for pretty grim reading; this one is no exception. Herbert Marcuse's *One-dimensional Man* described a totally administered world of people who identify with their home appliances. Henri Lefebvre wrote about the commodification of everyday life. But there was hope between the lines. For Marcuse, the technological means of enslaving people could, under different circumstances, liberate society from alienated labour and reorient the erotic base of culture towards the life instincts; eros, in other words. Lefebvre saw the city as a contradictory space of possibility. Paris in 1871, when the Communards transformed the centre into a short-lived experiment in self-determination; or in 1968, when students and workers became, for a brief time, the agents of history: these sparks of possibility coruscate today in the streets and on the squares of Cairo, Athens and New York. Walter Benjamin, Marxist critic of early 20th Century society, styled his life on the great 19th Century poet Charles Baudelaire, the archetypal *flaneur* stalking the Parisian streets and arcades. He said of Baudelaire: 'with each step, the walk takes on greater momentum; ever weaker grow the temptations of bistros, of shops, of smiling women, ever more irresistible the magnetism of the next street corner, of a distant square in the fog, of the back of a woman walking before him.'[7] Pleasures in which only the most affluent could indulge remind us of how unequal and unjust society is, and moreover, of what might be possible if class relations were overturned and the forces of production brought under common

ownership. Later the fantasy was rationalised, recycled and reduced to a standard that an emergent 'mass' consumer could afford. Arcades were bulldozed, and in their place the now-ubiquitous shopping mall rose.

Marcuse, Lefebvre and Benjamin were not the sort of critics to call upon people to tighten their belts. They recognised that humans are sensuous beings. They recognised, as Marx had before them, that in a society divided by relations of class, power, and privilege, sensuous life has been cut from the body and pasted to the commodity, priced beyond what so many can afford.

i, the non-commodified no-logo

The senses have been rained on by cluster bombs of commodities. Countries have become brands; cities have become supermarkets; homes have become show houses; people have become consumers. Logos turn into dollars. As Naomi Klein pointed out, logos are worth more than the material holdings of the companies they identify. Nike, for example, outsources production to manufacturers in low-wage economies and concentrates the bulk of their investment on creating brand awareness. The Nike swoosh logo has become a universally recognisable symbol of sportswear, training shoes, fitness, celebrity, quality and cool. Though what about that ubiquitous lower case i we associate with Apple products? It is a strange kind of sign which, unlike the swoosh, cannot be trademarked; it is property held in common that other companies can use, perhaps to grace their products and services with a little piece of that Apple magic. It is a signifier on the edge of the void, dancing with and between commodities, never becoming a billion-dollar logo tradable on stock markets. It is a commodity today and free-floating sign tomorrow, a symbol of the excessive little something that distinguishes the iPhone from an ordinary phone, iGoogle from ordinary Google. It is this excess that *iCommunism* proposes we wrest from the commodity altogether, to liberate pleasure from the shopping experience, from desire's dirty association with the market – consumerism - a system that survives through a constant turnaround of products bought and paid for by labour, the libido, and ultimately the planet.

The book does not battle against consumption per se, but rather the capitalist form of consumption to which desires have become knotted. The battle here is to wrest the i of Eros from the commodity and to transfer it to a word that evokes images of hardship and asceticism rather than abundance and joy. *iCommunism* unties the knot of capitalist production and subjective desire. It splits fetishism from commodity fetishism, use-value from exchange-value, and identifies an adaptive human nature in place of a selfish and instrumental nature; politics proper from the palliatives of ethical and eco-consumption.

Commune, the commons, community – whatever it signified in the past, communism is an open concept, an eternal Idea says Alain Badiou; an historical anchoring point 'of everything elusive, slippery and evanescent', [8] an idea which has demon-strated, in all-too-brief moments of liberation, the possibility of an alternative to the market economy; 'to parliamentary democracy – the form of state suited to capitalism – and the inevitable and 'natural' character of the most monstrous of inequalities.'[9] If ordinary communism is about equality, justice and self-determination, a socially owned and rationally planned economy, *iCommunism* is also about pleasure: the proposition that it is possible to create a material foundation for the universal liberation of the senses – of playfulness and an aesthetic life: that the 'excessive' flourishes upon functions (what the i signifies to the phone) is the joyfulness that justifies the sacrifices that we collectively need to make in order to realise a vision of communism wholly distinguishable from the nightmare worlds of capitalism and really existing socialism.

The book is organised into five short chapters on capitalism, consumption and the consuming subject. Chapter 1.0 *Addiction* is about desire and false needs, drawing on Marx, Lacan, Adorno and Horkheimer and others to offer some explanation as to how subjective desires and capitalism have become so bound together. 2.0 *Excess* discusses the economy and ecology, the uneven nature of consumption, divisions between rich and poor, and in particular, the environmental consequences of mass consumption. 3.0 *Identification* is about standardisation, the denigration of our freedoms and the emptiness of our choices, challenging the idea that the Internet liberates the consumer from the rationalised one-dimensionality of consumerism. 4.0 *Conscience* discusses ethical and ecological forms of consumption, questioning whether there is any ethical or ecological value whatsoever in individual gestures to reduce dependency on consumer products. 5.0 *Commons* is about liberation.

1.0 Addiction

Between wants and needs

What is a need? While there might be some disagreement among postmodernists, a materialist would argue that food is a need. What about art or love? Do we need science? Animals get by without it. Human needs are complex and not simply reducible to bodily functions. Yet people are constantly judged for buying things that exceed a narrow definition of need. Consumerist ideologies, which oppose any attempt to regulate consumption, are pitted against anti-consumerist ideologies advocating boycotts, self-sufficiency and so forth, strategies that do little more than make us feel good about ourselves while structurally changing nothing. This chapter explores the relationship between capitalism and desire, drawing on a number of theorists to offer an explanation as to why mass-marketed objects have such a hold over us. The aim is to discern a difference between fetishes and fetishised commodities; use-value and exchange-value; desire and self-interest; needs proper to humankind and needs, let us dare to say, that are false.

1.1 M-C-M^i
The strangest of fetishes are those that have been normalised

According to Freud, it is not need, as such, that motivates us but rather the anticipation of (libidinal) pleasure from the satisfaction of needs - if hungry we tend to think of a cooked meal rather than a raw cabbage and if thirsty a flavoured drink rather than a glass of water. Ejected from a womb that drip-feeds our desires, we enter a world in which desires are frustrated and gratifications delayed; a world in which the archetypal Father competes for the mother's attention. Rather than fixed biological categories, words such as father and mother can be thought of as linguistic placeholders that map power dynamics in a patriarchal society. The Father can be a sign for any social authority with the power to punish and the Mother the object of desire. In a society obsessed with consumption, consumer goods become fetishised objects of desire.

One of Freud's male patients developed a fetish for the shine on women's noses. The shine compensated for a fear of castration as according to Freud fetishes help men come to terms with the fact that women have no penis (woman is essentially 'castrated'). While other men go through all the bother of courtship before consummating their desire, the fetishist gets instant though fleeting gratification, in this case from the serendipitous effect of light on a reflective surface. 'Penis' signifies power or possession and 'castration' powerlessness or lack. The shine makes up for feelings of powerlessness, an object or substitute 'penis' that can triumphantly if only momentarily be possessed. There is a permanent tension here between possession and loss, a pleasure sustained by a disavowed fear like the frightened child who peeks through half-closed fingers at a scene they secretly delight in. Commodities possess their own shine: an equally fleeting, ultimately dissatisfying colour, shape and texture compensating for what, perhaps unconsciously, we feel to be lacking in our lives. They compensate for feelings of powerlessness and alien-ation, allowing us to forget for a moment the issues that weigh heavily on our minds.

We only buy things because they have a use to us, and while a shiny nose might be of 'use' to one person it has no use to another. Consumer goods possess a use-value for the person buying them – otherwise they would not want them - and an exchange-value or monetary price bearing little or no relation to their intrinsic or subjective value. The exchange-value does not account for the sacrifices made by so many people to bring goods and services to market. Yet despite what we know about working conditions in India or the carbon emissions of air freight, most of us have no choice other than to buy the cheapest equivalent item available. Our wages, our conditions of life, force this upon us. For everyone, price becomes the ultimate determinant of value, and so however we view it, what Marx called commodity fetishism hooks us all. Whatever our belief or desire, in a society enveloped in capitalist relations of exchange, it is impossible to avoid being active in those relations. Whatever we think about money, we are forced to act as if money possesses value. Commodities, whether the apples we eat or the Apples we surf the net on, are polished up by cheap labour. The shine that bounces off their surfaces dazzles and blinds us to the circumstances of their creation, the castrated human and environmental circuitry of real and virtual cornucopias. The fetish for commodities is universal and there is nothing – not even sessions on Freud's couch – that we can do about it, at least individually.

Human nature is an unfinished project

The commodity has vacuumed sensuous life from the fabric of being, leaving in its wake a husk of personality that the market has priced up; a husk of what Marx called our species being - the vital powers, dispositions, capacities and drives that distinguish humans from animals. As Marx said: 'what distinguishes the worst architect from the best of bees is that the architect builds the [honeycomb] cell in his mind before he constructs it in wax.'[1] We have become strangers to ourselves. In place of sensuality we see objects, we even see ourselves as commodities. Consider this advice to a job candidate from a career site:

> When a company is determining how to advertise their products to consumers, they focus on its unique selling points - the things which make the product different from any other. It may be that it is smaller, lasts longer or tastes better than its competitors. The same principle applies to you when you are applying for a new job.[2] (Monster.co.uk career advice)

We confront the market as free independent labourers forced to see ourselves as potential assets that capital can use up and discard when it no longer requires them. Alienation stems from the fact that the creative capacity, intellect and emotions of individuals are indexed to capital. Instead of work being a source of pleasure and spiritual satisfaction, it becomes a burden. The vital force of creation becomes an object of exchange as those around us become competitors grubbing about for jobs they probably deserve as much as we do. We reflect on ourselves, the capacities of the body, the emotions, drives and experiences that shape identity. But this becomes an instrumental process, most evident in how we construct our CVs: thinking about the skills employers want, the value of doing voluntary work, the benefits of the networks we belong to, and how personal attributes will affect job prospects. We are robbed of our social agency, acting only as agents of capital and seeing the world through its imagined eyes, justifying our place in society on its terms. Numbers dance around us. Is a university education value for money? – *Does it meet the needs of industry?* - Do the Greeks deserve a bailout? Has an immigrant earned the right to remain? Numbers degrade us. They price up personality, life experience and love. Even the planet has a price. CO_2 becomes an object of exchange through carbon trading schemes while the 'bill' for global warming is expected to reach £250 billion by 2050. States are spurred into action only when profit is jeopardised, the results rarely benefitting those who dwell in the flood plains.

Fredric Jameson writes, 'no society has ever been quite so addictive, quite so inseparable from the condition of addictiveness as this one, which did not invent gambling, to be sure, but which did invent compulsive consumption.'[3] The more life is commodified, the greater the need to compensate for the profound loss incurred to the individual and society in general, and the more, up to a point, we become addicted to consumption. We are locked into a vicious cycle of working in order to get the fix that compensates for our alienation.

Capitalism has tied the knot with Eros; the commodity is the glint in our loving eye

We turned stone into wheels and minerals into microchips, and in these processes of thought and creation a different kind of individual was cultivated, one irreconcilable with our forebears. But only a certain kind of nature is suited to capitalism at this intense 'late capitalist' phase of commodity production: a nature made to sweat for consumption.

Unless crafting them into a candle first, a candle-maker is unlikely to sell the materials she bought – the wax, wick and mould – for more than she paid for them. However, through the power of her labour she transforms wax into a candle and adds value to the materials purchased. Whether a shoe factory in Indonesia or a shoe shop in Inverness, every firm operates according to this principle. But whereas our self-employed candle-maker kept the additional value she created, the additional value the worker creates translates into profit or surplus-value for owners and shareholders, some of which is reinvested into expanding the business, taxation and diminishing surplus wages for workers to pay for diminishing surplus consumption. No matter how sophisticated the operation grows, it remains dependent on labour. Without labour machines are idle, materials go to waste and there is no opportunity to make profit. This is why strikes are so disruptive and governments so hostile to them. They literally stop capital in its tracks.

The whole process of capitalist accumulation is a circular and self-expanding motion from production through to consumption and back again. Marx called this cycle M-C-M'. When businesses invest money into commodities such as machinery and labour they speculate on making a higher return. The 'M' or money component of the formula is the investment that kicks off the cycle, the money to buy the wick, wax and mould, and the labour power that turns it all into a commodity 'C', the 'candle'. The wager is that a consumer will buy the candle or service or whatever, and if they do, money enters back into circulation, the second 'M' in the formula. So what does the dash after the second M represent? This is profit derived from labour, the surplus-value that enables capital not only to circulate but also to expand. The excess creamed off labour drives capitalism forward, enabling it to span the globe and absorb life to the point of exhaustion: killing, conquering and colonising. Lacan relates this endless process of capitalist accumulation of surplus-value to what he called surplus-enjoyment, the self-exploitation of libidinal drives: an excess of desire, a *jouissance* or pleasure derived when grasping for the shine but never, of course, capturing it.

We can think about the object of desire as a kind of spoiler. Consider the pleasure we get from going to the movies. The last things we want to hear before seeing a film are 'spoilers'. These are the crucial plot developments typically towards the end of the film when the mystery is revealed, such as the identity of the murderer in the crime thriller genre. The suspense (and therefore the satisfaction) would be 'spoiled' if we knew the identity in advance. The mystery and the bungling attempts of the detective to uncover it drives the narrative and sustains our enjoyment, the enjoyment of dissatisfaction. There is no pleasure after all in having the mystery prematurely revealed to us, hence why we call such revelations spoilers. Lacan extends this principle to subjectivity in general. (Dis)satisfaction derives from every frustrated attempt to uncover the identity, to possess the knowledge or object that drives our desire. We are driven by a desire to possess something that we feel to be lacking in our lives, the mystery, the missing thing, 'it', or *objet petit a* – shine - always beyond our grasp. Desire circulates around the missing thing, never quite capturing it. Surplus-enjoyment is the excessive insatiable drive that hits against the obstacle and gets off on it. Surplus-value is the objet petit a of capital, that little missing thing causing the mad destructive drive for profit and insatiable need for workers-cum-consumers to keep the entire circuit in motion. Without an actual consumer to consume the accumulated value, it cannot be translated into money or liquid assets to be used for expansion. It is essential for capitalism's survival that the consumer is ultimately dissatisfied with their purchases and so therefore has a perpetual need to consume more. Slavoj Žižek nicely illustrates the point with the example of caffeine-free Diet Coke, a product with no nutritional value and with a strange, bittersweet taste. Coke is marketed as empty, it literally is the Real Thing and now with Coca-Cola Zero the truth is in the branding. Žižek writes:

> The more Coke you drink, the thirstier you are; the more profit you make, the more you want; the more you obey the superego command [to enjoy], the guiltier you are [for failing to satisfy your desire and therefore the command to enjoy].[4]

The economic crisis puts a different spin on this. There is a more obvious material obstacle in the way of the perpetually delayed satisfaction of desire. Depressed wages and the lack of available credit stop us from buying the Coca-Cola equivalent in the first place. When the young, disenfranchised, unemployed - the invisible - riot on the streets of London, Manchester and other cities in reaction to police brutality, smashing a shop window and stealing the product is sometimes the most realistic solution to the satisfaction of a need that was long ago manufactured.

So bound are our pleasures with consumption that to be denied opportunities to consume and to consume excessively is, as is often said, like being denied a human right. Capitalism's drive for profit becomes knotted to the subjective drive for enjoyment. The entwinement is so tragic, so destructive and so empty. The problem is not that we desire 'excessively' but rather that what we desire has enslaved us to capital. Alienated in the first instance from our species being, we become cannibals to our own creations, first producing value in excess of remuneration in wage (surplus-value) and second by consuming value in an endless quest to satisfy a libidinal drive (surplus-enjoyment). Capitalism cannot survive without 'it' but the subject can survive – even flourish – without capitalism.

Today, though, it is hard to see through the fog of so-called consumer society and the myth that humans are merely selfish, wasteful, shallow, and destructively excessive. It is no wonder that the utopian imagination is so destitute when human nature is made to look so grubby. But a species that can design a rocket ship to fly to the moon is no more of an animal than a fish is a reptile. If a species can imagine flight and then build airplanes, it can imagine a better world and become the historical agent in the making of that world. It can overcome hardship and inequality, and it can create a sustainable environment in which all of us – Americans, Africans, Indians, Chinese – can thrive. Systems can be overturned when people confront their alienated condition, but cynicism prevails in the absence of a more benign notion of human nature.

Recovering use-value from relations of exchange entails the recovery of the vital, adaptive, thinking kernel of being and putting it to the service of our social needs rather than the needs of capital; in short it means recovering our humanity. It also means recovering a faith in a capacity all of us possess – perhaps even bankers and politicians – to transcend a condition born from the alienated relations that are, as Marx said, directly encountered and inherited from the past. It means having faith in humanity. Alain Badiou writes:

> If you think the world can and must change absolutely; that there is neither a nature of things to be respected nor preformed subjects to be maintained, you thereby admit that

the individual may be sacrificable. Meaning that the individual is not independently endowed with any intrinsic nature that would deserve our striving to perpetuate it.[5]

Defaults and dole queues are the collective hangover from a long consumer boom. But consumption remains the cure for overproduction and the individual palliative priced beyond the means of those in debt or on wages at the borderline of subsistence. Desire is still chasing the hair of the dog that bit us.

1.2 False Needs
There are needs and there are false needs and there are needed false needs

Our natures have changed. We cannot be satisfied with the desires of the archetypal cave dweller. We want more and we deserve it, collectively at least: needs, then, are historically contingent. Agrarian societies need shovels. A society rationalised in the interests of commerce needs Playstations. In 1957 Vance Packard published *The Hidden Persuaders,* a seminal work on the advertising industry. He cited a number of examples of how advertisers manufacture affinities between people and products. In one case, housewives were asked to report on which of three detergents they thought worked best, unaware that the only difference between them was the colour of the box. The detergent in the yellow box was reported to be too strong, the blue too weak and the one in the box coloured yellow and blue to be just right, 'wonderful' even. Goldilocks had found her porridge. The conclusion advertisers drew was that consumers make choices by discriminating *irrationally* between what are essentially the same products. We buy feelings rather than functions. Adorno and Horkheimer came to the same conclusion about the cultural manipulators they called the Culture Industry. Consumer goods, they said, are like mass-produced Yale locks, the difference between them 'measured in fractions of millimetres'.[6] The advertiser has turned miniscule differences into fetishes, and by identifying with differences that are essentially the same, we become a pallid version of the self: what Adorno and Horkheimer called a pseudo-individual, much like the 'one-dimensional man' of Marcuse who 'swallows up' her alienated existence by identifying with the things she consumes. Consider how the late Steve Jobs, the former CEO of Apple, pitched the iPhone 4:

> Now, this is really hot ... you got to see this thing in person, it's one of the most beautiful designs you've ever seen ... glass on the front and rear, stainless steel running around ... its closest kin is like a beautiful old Leica camera.

Jobs conjured an affinity between the subject and object, selling us a warm feeling; perhaps one we associate with childhood. The libido is wrapped into Apple's aesthetic. The reflective surface on the iPhone returns an image of the ego protected by the hard steel casing: an image of the Leica, protecting an otherwise fragile self. We were lost and now we recover our identity, only for it to disappear again – until reimagined in versions 5, 6 and 7.

The culture industry is not a particular set of manufacturers, but rather a broad range of cultural manipulators – including advertisers, the film industry and the mass media in general – which, in various ways, directly and indirectly, stoke and manipulate feelings of anxiety. They manufacture false needs, first by pointing out deficiencies we did not know we had, and then by providing solutions to them: a cream to heal blemishes, a stupid set of saucepans with which to impress dinner guests, a self-help guide for improving social skills. People are not passive dupes responding mechanically to media messages; 'they desire a deception which is nonetheless transparent to them', as Adorno wrote.[7] They desire the missing feeling, the warmth and love we all crave and others boring into the soul in simulated 3D appear to have found.

The culture industry is the machinery that does the job of connecting surplus-value with surplus-enjoyment, but on a mass scale – explaining why so many of us share the same fetishistic desire for certain consumer goods. By presenting objects as fillers for feelings of alienation and anxiety, this machinery connects capital's insatiable drive for profit with the subject's insatiable drive for satisfaction. And because everyone desires, regardless of how poor or wealthy they are, everyone can be made to feel deprived, to have a legitimate need for something. By manufacturing false needs the culture industry is able to make even the affluent feel deprived, feel the pinch of austerity by having to cut down on the designer labels that confirm their status in the eyes of significant others. Humans adapt to their environment and develop another kind of nature – a second nature. We have adapted to the demands of the culture industry. And so those who buy facile creams, have 'boob jobs', drive around in 'performance' vehicles, really do feel the need for them – really do feel inadequate without them. The addicted go to rehab, but rehab for the consumer is located in a different kind of society: one that is not penetrated by a culture industry or equivalent, not a society of 'mass deception', not Soviet Russia, not Nazi Germany, not sham liberal-parliamentary democracies.

While feelings of anxiety and inadequacy are not peculiar to capitalism, the global-scale manipulation of these feelings surely is. We can discern a difference between consumption under capitalism – in which that consumption fuels capitalist expansion and profit – and consumption in a society in which the means of production are socially owned and utilised for social and of course individual needs. Would women in a communist society feel inadequate over their breast size or men their sexual performance? Almost certainly. But would so many people experience these same anxieties and need a particular product to compensate for them, the wonder drug, the wonder bra or the wonder car?

People will always want to live in beautiful homes and dress in ways that others find aesthetically pleasing. But there is a difference between this desire and an ego whose sense of self is secure only when accumulating stuff; whose aesthetic judgements are determined by fashion alone.

M-C-M^i is the formula of consumerism

The farmer has stumbled into one of the more affluent parts of town. His peasant tunic is swapped for a designer sweater. The produce he sells is fresh and organic and the logos emblazoned on them endorse the authenticity of his claim of having been kind to the soil, chickens and hired hands. Planet organic is a utopia in embryo, a utopia that comes at a price few can afford. Only in a society where 5-a-day is an aspiration, not a reality, can such a smorgasbord of earthly delights be so desirable and yet so exclusive. The fresh lettuce, the organic tomato, the state-of-the-art gadget, the street cool and the ubiquitous i plucked from the hand and heart are quickly transported to market before they go rotten. The i has become the symbol of freshness, cool, individuality, information, that little bit of extra something, the mystery – *objet petit a* – that drives our desire. It is the surplus-value stolen from the worker, the Apple polished and fetishised for consumption, the shine on the nose of commodities: the i of Eros. The excess of capital becomes bound up with the excess of human desire which together fuel consumerism represented here by the formula M-C-M^i. It is a bind that needs untying if the excess of human desire is to be liberated and become *productive* creative excess no longer connected to the instrumental demands of capital. The human and environmental impact of the bind that entwines surplus-value and surplus-enjoyment, and the uneven nature of consumption, is the focus of the next chapter.

2.0 Excess

The advertising slogans for Pepsi-Cola sound out above the collapse of continents (Adorno and Horkheimer)
Let us put excessive consumption into perspective and give it an identity, first with a little preamble from the Russian literary theorist Mikhail Bakhtin. In the novels of Rabelais, Bakhtin wrote, the peasantry celebrated the end of the harvest with a 'banquet for all the world'. Their produce resulted from the collective efforts of an entire community, a common wealth exceeding the harvest of individual labour. The banquet was therefore a celebration of a body that had transgressed its material limits. By contrast the banquets of bourgeois literature celebrated:

> the contentment and satiety of the selfish individual, his personal enjoyment, and not the triumph of the people as a whole... it is no longer the "banquet for all the world," in which all take part, but an intimate feast with beggars at the door.[1]

No longer touching base with the collective efforts of community, excess has gotten a bad name. Restaurants in the UK close at a rate of 100 per month, while the Taybarns buffet chain is taking the restaurant industry by storm with their recession busting slogan: 'Enjoy as much as you like, as many times as you like. All for one fixed price!' The all-you-can-eat buffet is the modern equivalent of the medieval banquet, now symbolising a socially disconnected individual: a body that has been politically, economically, socially and culturally denuded. One customer explains why buffets are so compulsive: "When I come here I pig out. I feel like I have to because there's such a selection and I don't want to miss out".[2] Fear lingers between the lines. The peasant feared the elements, the modern worker fears being priced out of the market and losing out on a good deal, relative of course to their income. We have all become beggars at the door, the door of international finance, grasping in vain for a piece of the highlife captured in the Boxing Day sale refrain: 'I am desperate to get a Gucci handbag'.[3] The all-you-can-eat buffet is the banquet at the end of the world.

Excessive consumption is obviously a relative concept. It is when we compare the excesses of the dominant elite to the blowouts of the Tayburn's customer that matters are brought into perspective. Thorstein Veblen's fin de siècle classic *Conspicuous Consumption* was about bourgeois ostentation. Today's elites display their wealth on a scale that exceeds that of the Pharaohs with their pyramids and the Victorians with their town halls. Today, reflective towers rise above the clouds in Dubai, Mumbai and Shanghai, ostentations of one class that to another languishing in their shadows is mere obscenity. While cheap laughs are had observing the vulgarity of the working class in the freak shows of reality TV, little compares to the vulgarity at Bugis Junction, Singapore, where a US $1 million diamond-studded Christmas tree is on seasonal display; a fraction of the cost of the US $11.4m tree at the Emirates Palace hotel. The super-rich can buy a floating Monaco featuring scaled-down versions of the Monte Carlo Casino and racetrack,[4] while the once-affluent consumer is slung out of their home in Florida.[5] In an alternate but all too familiar reality, the first '$1 Billion Home' with its 27 storeys of opulence rises over the squalor of Mumbai.[6]

The contrasts between the consumption of one class and that of another are so great that they lead us to question why the phrase 'consumer society' is used with such abandon. Most people in the 'big society' played no part in the decision-making processes that led to the global financial crisis. Most of us have no voice in the affairs of state or self-determination in the workplace. For many people consumption is an aspiration not a reality. The consumer society is more than convenient shorthand for describing a norm; it is an ideological device that turns all consumers – whether they live on the mean streets of Baltimore or the leafy avenues of the Hamptons – into one another's equivalents, thereby disguising the economic and political power that divides them. Consumption is a class issue. This chapter is on the material divisions and social and environmental consequences of the capitalist form of consumption.

2.1 Blow Out
There is no such thing as scarcity; austerity prevails

In 2010 the anonymous blogger 'Austerity Mum', later revealed to be the millionaire Lisa Unwin, made headlines with her advice on how to survive the recession. This was the year when austerity, defined as 'forced or extreme economy', was the Merriam-Webster Dictionary's most widely searched word.[7] Austerity is necessary when trekking across the desert with only a flask of water. Late capitalism is no desert though; shelves are stacked high and warehouses are overflowing. The only quantity in short supply is the consumer. In this world of absurdities, deserts of scarcity are manufactured. Within them are oasis enclaves gushing with water on tap and supermarket shelves groaning with bottles of water taken from distant springs.

Among the sins of the industrialised model of food consumption is the spread of diabetes and rising levels of obesity wherever fast food chains get a foothold. 350 million people around the world today are diabetic.[8] These are boom times for the fitness industry, the dieting industry, and now the gastric bypass surgery industry. Stomach stapling, according to one US clinic, can shave off as much as 200 pounds; a necessary measure in a country where 300,000 people die from symptoms of morbid obesity every year. This contrasts starkly to developing countries where 27-28% of all children are underweight or stunted through malnutrition.[9] In private consumption, the wealthiest 20% of the global population consume 76.6% of all consumable goods, while the poorest 20% consume just 1.5%.[10] All consumers are equal but some can make austerity a lifestyle choice.

Austerity chic was the fashion of 2008. Fearful of bumping into a picket line of redundant workers, the sensitive 'recessionista' ditched the 'bling' for dark coloured cashmeres lying idle in the closet.[11] While the masses had been shaken, they had not been stirred – and so seasons change, with springtime coming early for some. In the first quarter of 2010, a 13% jump in sales of Louis Vuitton handbags took 'analyst's breath away' according to the *Guardian*. Good news comes in spades. The world's biggest luxury consumer firm LVMH saw champagne sales jump 20%; watch and jewellery sales also soared by 34%.[12] The luxury goods sector is recession-proof; as one newspaper columnist put it: 'rich people might be ruthless and smug, but they make terrific customers.'[13]

The poorer countries of the world have to produce 40% more goods today than they did in 1977 to purchase the equivalent from richer countries.[14] In an era of combined and uneven consumption, the evident disparity in purchasing power between nations cuts across all societies: 'consumer' and 'producer' alike.

Take China, for example – the great white hope of the 21st Century – sliding down the UN human development index ever since the start of its economic miracle (we never hear the phrase social miracle). China ranks 92nd in the index, while Cuba, a country crippled by a half-century-long US trade embargo, ranks 52nd.[15] And the 'factory of the world' is likely to remain just that – a factory – with no mass consumer society on the horizon, given that 1.3 billion of its people eke out an existence on an average of just $285 a year.[16] And so by producing more than it consumes, China simply adds to the heap of goods western consumers can no longer afford to purchase.

Let us pose the question: are we really 'all in this together', as

David Cameron suggests? Do we need to make a 'shared sacrifice' as Barack Obama tells us? Not according to the American Right. As Rush Limbaugh put it when defending the excesses of the rich, 'we do not believe in shared sacrifice! ...– once again, I think the guy is losing it!'[17] The Left could learn something here.

There is always a crisis of consumption

The roots of the current economic crisis can be traced back to before neoliberalism and the relaxation of restrictions on the free-flow of financial capital. The crisis is a result of a longer-term structural crisis of over-accumulation, too much stuff produced for too little demand. As unemployment and underemployment increases, jobs become less secure and there is a downward pressure on wages, further undermining consumer demand. Credit was a temporary solution to wage repression, as it allowed those affected to borrow money – in effect to keep capital in circulation. Credit gave substance to the claim that we live in a consumer society.

The figures on the transfer of wealth from the poorest to the richest provide some background to our dependence on credit. In 1979 the richest 1% of the UK population owned 8.9% of the wealth. By 2006 the figure was 22.8%.[18] The poorest quarter of American households survive on about $50 a day, at least 40% or more of this wealth services interest on debt.[19] As a consequence of neoliberalism, wages have been squeezed as productivity levels rise, with the financial sector siphoning off chunks in the form of interest payments. With a significant amount of productive output geared towards mass consumption, the super-rich still depend on a buoyant consumer market for their wealth. However, the institutions and laws that protected wages, working conditions and welfare have been systematically dismantled by neoliberal regimes. This has not only made people more vulnerable, but has also threatened the survival of the consumerist model of capitalist accumulation. Simply put, people no longer have the purchasing capacity to 'spend their way' out of recession. George W. Bush, worried about the economic downturn after the 9/11 attacks, was in a position to say 'Get out there and shop. It's the American way' because the US Fed under Alan Greenspan could reduce interest rates on loans and expect a consumer boom to result.[20] Such calls fall on deaf ears when there is no credit or wage capacity to finance loans.

By 2007 total personal debt in the US was around $14,374.5 billion[21] and in the UK around £1,457 billion.[22] The average family debt in the UK is now expected to reach £77,000 by 2015.[23] While the very wealthiest lost £155 billion worth of assets during the crash, a year later the combined wealth of the richest 1,000 people in the UK rose by a record breaking 30%.[24] The poorest households bore the brunt of the crisis. Since the crash, unemployment has soared in the US and UK. By 2011, before the cull in public sector jobs came into effect, there were 2.4 million unemployed in the UK, the highest figure since 1984.[25]

There are stories behind these figures that are never told, stories about immigrants forced into prostitution; single mothers juggling two jobs to support a family; graduate students on low-paid contracts with few prospects of permanent work; highly skilled and experienced professionals made redundant at the prime of their working lives; those requiring care forced onto the streets and those compensating for cuts in public services by working longer hours to provide crucial services. There are the underemployed, contract and casual workers. There is nothing left to sacrifice here, not for the economy or even for the planet.

2.2 Capitocene
The geological age of capital

From Kyoto to Copenhagen, the aggregate amount of carbon emissions pumped into the atmosphere has risen year on year, a trend bucked only in 2009 when the global economy was in a recession.[26] 2010 made up for this though with the largest yearly output of carbon emissions on record, leading the International Energy Agency to declare that global warming can no longer be contained at safe levels.[27] James Hansen has warned of ecological tipping points, such as the melting Arctic sea ice or the release of methane from Siberia's frozen tundra that would cause amplifying and unpredictable feedbacks throughout the entire biosphere. The human impact on the environment is now thought so great as to equate to what happened to the dinosaurs when an asteroid plunged into the Gulf of Mexico at the end of the Cretaceous period. Now for the first time in Earth's history biological life is triggering a mass extinction event ushering a new geological age called the Anthropocene.

Humans have been around for 1000s of years. Yet it is only in the past 200 or so years with the development of capitalism and large-scale industry that sustainability has become a planetary wide issue. Industrial development has not in itself led to this condition but rather the unplanned and exploitative manner in which the forces of production are utilised for the purposes of securing private gain. The capitalist mode of production is sustained through expansion and expands by using up human and natural resources disrupting the established harmony between humans and nature causing what Marx called a metabolic rift. The problem then with the term Anthropocene – anthro as in human – is that it signifies humans in general as the destructive cause of rising carbon emissions. It implies that we are all 'in it together', that we all, by definition of being human, share an equal responsibility for the state of the environment and all therefore have to make sacrifices, take fewer flights or, if you happen to live in Africa, have fewer babies. These are sacrifices, in other words, for sustaining capitalism with an eco-friendly face. But it needs to be remembered that most of us have little determination over our lives, least of all the economy, and those few who can afford to make conscientious decisions about what or how much they consume are not going to have any effect on aggregate levels of carbon emissions by 'going green' or, for that matter, living amongst nature eating nuts and berries. It is not then the human species as such that causes global warming but a specific mode of production, accumulation and exchange. The capitalist laws of motion set in train an extinction event, the extinction of species, industries, livelihoods, communities and hope. At the speed of a juggernaut, no an asteroid, capitalism blisters the earth, sets forests aflame and triggers metaphorical earthquakes and tsunamis. It has forced scarcity upon the planet's inhabitants, the fish of the open seas, animals of the open plains, people of the enclosed commons, in order to preserve the wealth and power of a tiny elite, less even than 1% of the global population. This is not a geological age triggered by an indeterminate human but rather the geological age of capital, the Capitocene. Without a change in the social relations of production profit will always trump planet and the technological means to address global warming and end a condition of scarcity will be squandered.

Scarcity is an excuse, Marcuse wrote, that since its inception has justified institutional repression, but 'weakens as man's knowledge and control over nature enhances the means for fulfilling human needs with a minimum of toil.'[28] But the excuse still convinces. Scarcity of jobs becomes a problem of immigration, scarcity of credit a problem of individual greed and scarcity of natural resources a problem of overpopulation. As long as there is capitalism there is no end to scarcity, no end to the need for austerity. The ideology that humans are the cause not a mode of production that survives by constantly expanding and exhausting nature, putting entire habitats at risk, killing off cultures, destroying communities, must be challenged. If not, it really is easier to imagine the end of the world than the end of capitalism, as Fredric Jameson puts it.

The car, that symbol of freedom, that extension of the person-ality, that penis substitute, has a lot to answer for here. Over 650 million cars are estimated to be on the streets today. According to Ivan Illich, gridlocked traffic has meant that the average American travels at around 5 miles per hour, putting in an average of 1,600 hours to travel 7,500 miles. As fossil fuels are pumped into the atmosphere to build, import, maintain, run and dispose of cars, wars are fought for access to the diminishing supplies of oil needed in factories and petrol stations. According to the International Energy Agency oil will 'peak' in about 2020, after which supplies will rapidly diminish. Roads carve up our cities, destroying natural and social habitats. The flaneur is stopped in his tracks, unable to wander the city without being constantly alert as to the flow of traffic and the recklessness of frustrated drivers impatient to get to their destination. The infra-structure of social life, from work through to leisure, communi-cation, and consumption, is rationalised for car use. It is entirely *rational* then that people choose to drive cars given the practical-ities of getting around cities where the infrastructure is designed for them. And, by the same token, it is entirely *irrational* that cities are structured and maintained for cars, especially in view of what we now know about the environmental consequences. The irrationality of the whole – the infrastructure - begets the ratio-nality of the part – driving cars because it is practical to do so. When society is incapable of thinking beyond a world of concrete arteries, the environmental cost of maintaining the car industry becomes a factor when calculating the planetary resources needed to sustain a 'lifestyle' forced upon us. According to the World Wildlife Fund's 2010 *Living Planet Report*, 1.5 planets are needed to support current levels of consumption and absorb CO_2 waste. Assuming there is not a global depression in the meantime or, dare we imagine, a transformation of the mode of production, the figure is expected to rise to two planets by 2030.[29]

What about the gadgets we love so much and have become so

dependent on? Even if we are not seduced into purchasing an iPad 2 less than a year after the iPad 1 was released, it is difficult to avoid updating perfectly serviceable electronic goods when they no longer meet a general industrial standard. We need faster processors, bigger flash memory and more advanced graphics chips to cope with all the information on which we now depend for our work. In 2007, the three-billionth cell phone was manufactured. Containing toxic materials such as lead and mercury, electronic goods make up 70% of toxic waste in US landfills.[30] But it is the human cost of consumption that most graphically illustrates the problem with an economic model whose health thrives on a constant turnaround of product. Coltan, for example, which is processed into a heat-resistant metal powder called tantalum, is used in mobile phones and computer chips. Quantities are found in the northeast region of the Congo where, according to the UN and human rights groups, many thousands of people have been massacred and displaced for access to the much sought-after commodity.[31]

In-built obsolescence and waste, supermarkets in New Zealand selling Kiwifruit from Italy, these are not the result of consumer demand *per se*; but of deregulated economies of scale that have come about because corporations (many of which are located in the west) need to expand in order to remain profitable. Everything begins with production and ends in consumption. As Marx said, 'a definite production determines a definite consumption, distribution and exchange as well as *definite relations between these different moments.*'[32] In order to be able to eat a cake we have to bake it first.

Global warming from this perspective is not a natural phenomenon, nor is it the result of individual greed. The consumer who buys a car to get to work, electronic devices to communicate, and food at prices they can afford is acting rationally (not necessarily unthinkingly) within a system that has become irrational to the point of threatening the natural environment upon which we depend. Even the capitalist who has to source the cheapest goods and labour to remain profitable is not generally in a position to be able to go 'carbon neutral'. The costs would be prohibitive and, considering the entire network of connections from extraction through to production, distribution, exchange, consumption and ultimately waste, practically impossible without massive state investment and regulation. Even then we would need to account for the environmental cost of manufacturing sustainable technologies on the required scale. With the narrative and predictions on global warming centring on human causes, Hollywood, with its penchant for dystopian and apocalyptic storylines, has written the script of our demise. It fits the scientific predictions on global warming to the scenario of the unchanging global order that we seem unable to think past, its spectacular sideshows are products of this conditioning. As with Hollywood's apocalyptic scripts, the means of producing global warming is privately owned but the solutions are foisted onto the individuated individual.

The Khan Hypothesis

The only good environmentalist is a dead one and the greatest of all was the Mogul warrior Genghis Khan. As the *Daily Mail* reported, Khan killed so many people "that large areas of cultivated land grew thick once again with trees, which absorb carbon dioxide from the atmosphere... ecologists believe it may be the first ever case of successful manmade global cooling."[33] Misanthropy has become respectable. It becomes self-evident that, because humans have caused global warming, humanity itself is the problem. This simultaneously justifies the anti-humanist ideologies common among environmentalists who want to return to a more primitive state, and the neoliberals who believe humans to be motivated by self-interest alone – an ideology that claims empathy, compassion and self-sacrifice disguise ulterior motives. The solution then shifts onto the individual, and in a game of pass-the-parcel with death as the prize, the winner is Africa. The Khan Hypothesis that population control is the solution to global warming begins at the birthplace of humanity.

It took until the beginning of the 19th Century for the global population to reach its first billion. It took a little over a decade, until 2011, for the population to rise from 6 to 7 billion. But this is not the reason why carbon emissions have risen so fast. The environmental campaigner George Monbiot notes that between 1980 and 2005 the population of Sub-Saharan Africa increased by 18.5%, but carbon emissions in the region over the same period rose by just 2.4%. In the same timeframe, the population of North America increased by 4% while carbon emissions in the region rose by as much as 14%. It is reported that carbon emissions in China now exceed those of the United States; but what is not so widely acknowledged when discussing China in this context is that a significant amount of its productive output is geared to western demands. When we factor in the unequal levels of consumption in the West, and that mass consumption, waste and obsolescence are unavoidable symptoms of the economic model, it is plain that the issue is capitalism itself. Yet a Malthusian logic persists. Malthus's concern was not overpopulation as such, but rather that rising populations would eat into the rich man's cake. As John Bellamy Foster et al. explain, the population argument 'is all about making mass consumption and hence the ordinary consumer (not the wealthy few) the culprit.'[34]

Overpopulation.org and Population Action International are typical examples of pressure groups that link western consumerism with global warming while at the same time placing considerable emphasis on population control in developing countries. On their website, under the heading 'what works' the former lists a range of ideas all linked to birth control in developing countries: family planning, education for girls and women, and so forth. The latter 'demonstrates how demographic variables relate to climate change vulnerability, and expands the concept of climate change resilience by highlighting critical gender, fertility, and reproductive health dimensions'.[35] Responsibility for global warming is displaced onto the poor, destitute and disenfranchised, who become carriers of a disease for which the vaccine is western-style family planning. Here, the register shifts away from the species itself and onto a specific kind of species: the black African.

But it is true nonetheless that if the consumption levels enjoyed by the 'average' western consumer (with their car, computer and IKEA furniture) were also enjoyed by everyone else around the world, the effect on the environment would likely be disastrous. In a question and answer session for the *Guardian* newspaper, the respected economic columnist Larry Elliot was asked whether consumerism as the solution to the economic crisis will eventually lead to ecological catastrophe. His typically measured answer was as follows:

Developing countries want the level of consumption we enjoy, people in the West have no great desire to consume less, and there is no real mass political movement advocating the sort of changes that would help.[36]

He is right of course. Remembering that it is the whole that is irrational rather than the part, the obvious solutions are those least palatable in a free-market society: those, essentially, that structurally impact upon the free-flow of capital. Consider again the example of the motorcar. A meaningful solution for bringing down carbon emissions is for governments around the world to invest massively in public transport and infrastructure, and end the effective subsidy to the motorcar industry. Consumers would no longer need to be 'persuaded' to leave their gas-guzzling SUVs at home; driving around the city would be unnecessary and, as in pedestrian streets, impossible. Instead General Motors is bailed out to the tune of US $50 billion, a positive intervention in many respects given the knock on effects on jobs in the material economy were the company to go under. Instead of re-orienting production, focus shifts to panaceas of technological environmentalism such as the carbon-free motorcar diverting the issue back onto the consumer. But as Jane Holtz Kay points out, the actual running of a car makes up a third of car-related carbon emissions. Another third is taken up in production and another third in its ultimate disposal.[37] Add the cost in building and maintaining roads as well as the broader infrastructure of priva-tised transportation, out of town supermarkets and so on, and the relative cost to the environment in actually running a car is even lower. By examining the whole cycle from production through to consumption, we realise that there are so many indus-tries and processes involved in bringing the things we consume to market that anything we do individually – whether it be recycling tin cans or driving around in hybrid cars – is effectively useless, an argument supported by the fact that global carbon emissions continue to rise. We return to eco-consumption in chapter 4.0 Conscience.

It is psychologically and politically important that we distin-guish human nature from naturalised capitalism, to shift the signifier from Anthropocene to Capitocene thus specifying where in the world the problem lies and then take effective measures to deal with it. The next chapter treads a familiar path that critiques of consumption traverse, with examples of how the individuated individual is wrapped in the consumerist aesthetic.

3.0 Identification

Variety has colonised the senses

The Parisian arcades held such wonders for Benjamin; would he have found the extensive maze of streets and boulevards that now house all the delights of the world so enchanting? Would he see a charming little French café on Place St-Michel or only the Ben & Jerry's sign among the decadent flourishes? Variety is a brand that colonised the city in preparation for the tourist onslaught. We shop and we surf, we buy ready-made and tailor-made, consume as we please and now, if what is said about the Internet had any truth to it, produce as we please. Variety implies choice, choice agency and agency freedom. Pleasure effervesces along this plane; somewhere along the way we discover our identity and the alienation we feel is blunted. Choice is a paradox, argues Renata Salecl. The more choices we have, the greater our anxiety about what to buy. And choice is socially mediated. We never buy simply 'for ourselves' but always in degrees for others. We are guided by fashions, the tastes of signif-icant others – our friends, workmates, family – the idea we have of ourselves, or rather the self we see reflecting back at us in the mirror. Why do we buy particular cars, phones or styles of clothes? Why do only certain clothes 'suit' us? Clothes probably say more about us than anything else we buy, which is why we are so careful when purchasing them. Even those who claim not to be 'fashion conscious' want their choices confirmed before parting with their cash. It might be the assistant from whom they seek approval, or a lover; ultimately, though, it is the reflection in the changing room mirror that nods an okay. We invest in what Lacan called an Imaginary double: an idea about the self that suits our own self-perception. It is a fantasy of how we imagine, or would like to imagine, others see us. Whenever we place significance on a particular brand or style we imagine ourselves to be compatible with it. Louis Althusser linked the Imaginary to ideology; what he called interpellation is that moment when we mis/recognise ourselves as the subject of a hailing object or authority. Things 'hail us' and as they do we make a beeline towards them thus negotiating our way past the plethora of choices on display.

The usual narrative about consumerism is that things changed after the 1960s, when new technologies and organisational methods combined with a growing demand for individual autonomy and self-expression; a demand that business could now satisfy using more flexible production methods to produce a greater variety of goods and services. Zygmunt Bauman is typical of many commentators who saw this as a shift from what he describes as a 'heavy, solid and condensed' Fordist mass production employing large numbers of workers to a lighter, 'liquid', networked 'post-Fordist' small-scale production employing far fewer workers. Not only did this give rise to a new form of organisation, it also (according to such arguments) gave rise to a new kind of subject; no longer a bureaucratic one-dimensional conformist, but instead an emotionally expressive, sophisticated and discerning individual. So from this perspective, the more 'totalising' views of those who claimed that homogeneity prevails and people have become one-dimensional are false. If anything, the thesis, associated with the Frankfurt School of Critical Theorists, especially Adorno, Horkheimer and Marcuse, is more relevant than ever.

We might be immune to certain gimmicks of the culture industry, though not all of them. With more variety it is more likely that there will be objects that speak to even the most discerning and eccentric of characters. Commerce captures us in the little things from which we derive meaning, almost as if the goods and services really were tailor-made to our whims and fancies. It is impossible to discern an identity that has not already been conceived in a book, advertising slogan, pop video, television series, blockbuster movie or YouTube clip. Every customer is king, a king of a culture that rings like tinnitus: the ring of pop jingoes wherever we go, the ring of the production line along which Manchester, Bristol and Leeds – retrofitted with Starbucks and Subways – tumble.

Choice has been sullied, individuality fetishised. This chapter is about a consumerist identity, the forced choices and false freedoms, an individuality becoming evanescent on the net of infinite variety, punching in a few words, sticking up a few photos, cobbling together sounds and images, fashioning a one-dimensionality as a marker of agency. The socio-cultural examples given here are perhaps the more familiar ones we often associate with consumption, the individualistic excesses that appear, if anything, as the negative manifestations of a society utterly beholden to commerce.

3.1 Enjoy Division
That we enjoy ourselves is no marker of our freedom

It is easy to identify moments of pleasure as a confirmation of our freedom to do as we please in a society that does indeed, at times, deliver the goods. If we are having a good time nothing seems forced. In the book *Fathers and Sons*, Ivan Turgenev wrote: 'time (as we all know) sometimes flies like a bird and sometimes crawls like a snail; but man is happiest when he does not even notice whether time is passing quickly or slowly.'[1] Time is slow when being jostled at bars by men swilling their drinks over you: when screaming to friends in an attempt to make conversation as the swaggering DJ places discs on his player as if painting onto a canvas the 21st Century equivalent of Picasso's *Les Demoiselles d'Avignon*. It is when time is neither fast nor slow, when we lose ourselves in the moment, that we are least cognisant of the world around us. When we enjoy ourselves there is no authority standing over us. When we consume we enjoy 'free time'.

Today the superego – that infernal internalised authority

making obscene demands - has censored the censor; the superego, as Lacan put it, permits us to enjoy, to do as we please, to do it without delay, and even to feel guilty for *not* having a good time. Marcuse called this liberation of desire repressive desublimation. Desublimation is another word for instant gratification, a gratification that is fleeting and superficial, a gratification with a price tag, making the satisfaction of desire ever more subject to wage labour – or cheap credit – as the only means of getting what we want; one of the reasons why desublimated pleasure is repressive under these conditions at least.

We cannot be forced to enjoy ourselves, but still enjoyment is, in many respects, forced. Those moments when only other people are having fun are times, perhaps, when we are more acutely aware of our alienation, more acutely aware of the rituals and codes of every day life which pressurise us to perform in certain ways. Anxiety gnaws the ego, causing us to reflect on whether there is something wrong with us if we are not enjoying ourselves too. In these moments we feel part of what David Riesman called the lonely crowd. Jean Baudrillard wrote:

> It is no longer desire, nor even 'taste' nor a specific preference which are at issue, but a generalised curiosity driven by a diffuse obsession, a *fun morality*, whose imperative is enjoyment and the complete exploitation of all the possibilities of being thrilled, experiencing pleasure, and being gratified.[2]

The Fun at Work Company is typical of many online sources proselytising fun, here with advice on how to improve workplace collegiality:

> A smile costs nothing and makes everybodys [sic] day ... but have some of us forgotten how? Our theatre director will teach your staff that 'natural' smile without the cheesy grin.

These are fun workshops that everyone can enjoy.

In certain circumstances, donning a clownish outfit can be subversive, such as when creating a dissonance with uniformed police whose arms are locked in a chain to circulate and suffocate protesters. But it is also a device that businesses and politicians deploy to defuse the seriousness of the issues they highlight, the BBC's Comic Relief being a case in point. From the website:

> All this funny business unites the whole nation in trying to make a difference to the lives of thousands of people living in abject poverty, or facing terrible injustice, both across Africa and in the UK.

If we are having a good time, if we are forgetting time, think time is suspended. The tortured and imprisoned have Amnesty International's 'Party for Human Rights' to support them; the poor and the dispossessed have 'Comic Relief'; the planet has 'Earth day' celebrated with Greenpeace, Starbucks and General Motors.

Parties that are greater than countries

Enjoyment is coded and ritualised, beginning in one country and quickly spreading to others. Invented traditions, the social historian Eric Hobsbawm wrote, are any set of practices governed by rules and rituals of a symbolic nature, constituting a general norm. Invented traditions aim to inculcate 'certain values and norms of behaviour by repetition which automatically implies continuity with the past.'[3] The genealogy of such rituals is often contested. But with the development of mass global media, traditions in one country travel quickly to another, becoming international in character, with their source readily identifiable. Coca-Cola, for example, did not (as is often thought) invent the plump old man in a red uniform we now identify as

Santa Claus, but it did popularise him through its 1930s advertising campaign.

The culture industry does not simply pluck ideas out of thin air; Adorno wrote that it fuses the old and familiar, reproducing, reinventing and amplifying rituals, fusing them with the latest trends. 122 million Americans are estimated to have celebrated St Patrick's Day in 2011, spending around $4.14 billion.[4] Valentine's Day raked in just under $14.7 billion.[5] Feeling the pinch of austerity is Easter, in decline though still managing to net around $12.73 billion.[6] Trumping them all, of course, is the holiday season, when Americans spend around $451.5 billion according to the US National Retail Federation.[7] If the holiday season in the US were a country, its revenue as GDP would make it the 26th richest country in the world.[8]

Weddings also make good business. The 2011 Royal Wedding cost Britain an estimated £20 million, a figure that the global elites are struggling to keep up with. The government in India is now intervening to curb a trend among the rich to outdo one another with more and more lavish displays of ostentation: elephants, the Bolshoi Ballet, a fleet of aircraft to jet guests to and from the destination every hour. Love knows no limits. The wedding industry in the UK is worth around £5.5 billion annually, helped in part by the now-burgeoning 'Stag and Hen' industry. The hen night customer can enjoy pole dancing: 'the emphasis is on having fun and that's what your hen weekend is all about.'[9] For the stag do there's 4x4 driving: 'why not feel all macho on your stag weekend and hop behind the wheel of a 4x4 – we guarantee you'll love it!'[10] Images of sex tourism and extreme sports alternate on the stagweekends.com homepage; these marry the bride to the groom.

Blackshirts to blue

Throughout the last week of June 2011, workers in Greece went on strike, the *Indignati* protested, the Euro went into free-fall, and parliaments capitulated to international finance. Then it was Saturday, June 25th to be precise: Global Smurfs Day. In London, Moscow and Athens, people came together to celebrate the 'Largest Gathering of People Dressed as Smurfs within a 24-hour Period in Multiple Venues'. In Spain, an entire village was painted blue. A month later, on July 28, the Smurfs rang the Wall Street opening bell; within a week, the Dow Jones Index dropped by 1000 points.

Politics and consumption juxtapose one another and merge. On Saturday there are street parties for a royal wedding and on Sunday there are parties across America celebrating the state-backed assassination of Osama Bin Laden by what Obama euphemistically called the 'raid team'.[11] In worlds populated by Smurfs, global warming can be fun. Ice Land Water Park in the UAE is a fantasy landscape of a desert country transformed by the melting of polar icecaps into a paradise of plastic ice and penguins.[12]

Žižek argues that the term 'proto-Fascism' is a lazy concept for avoiding conceptual analysis.[13] It is lazy when no examples are cited as evidence of such a tendency to warn of the dangers we face. Politically, we might cite as evidence the erosion of civil liberties, increasingly overt police brutality, rendition and 'pre-emptive' warfare as well as the rise of movements such as the Tea Party. Culturally, we might cite as evidence the individualism, ideological relativism, spectacle and the debasing and debilitating effect that consumerism has on the senses in general. The consumerist culture ringing like tinnitus – the awful and omnipresent commercialism, the smiley face, the blue costume - is the noise that threatens finally to deafen us.

3.2 Consumption for Dummies
Consumption does not come naturally; we have to be taught how to consume

Our lives are spent trying to satisfy the ambiguous demands of others, and so when there are so many choices we need some guidance, a clue here, a bit of advice there. The *Royal Wedding for Dummies*, published before the marriage in 2011 of Prince William and Kate Middleton, provided us with tips on how to celebrate the event. Getting in early to help toddlers form an identity, Marie Claire France recently launched *Marie Claire Enfants*, 'mode 40 pages pour les 3-12 ans' accompanied by a now inevitable Facebook site. The so-called consumer society has become the form or general framework structuring desire; in psychoanalytic terms the fantasy frame of desire, a Maze littered with pills for Pac-man to consume. But this society 'is no unidentifiable "ghost"', wrote Marcuse: 'it has its empirical hard core in the system of institutions, which are the established and frozen relationships among men.'[14] It is the theme park, the shopping mall, the supermarket and the state.

Newness is jarring. I remember when mobile phones first became available and looking on in disapproval as people using these devices sat together around tables, but engaged in separate conversations. Soon though, I was holding one, and by now they are an indispensible part of my life – or so it seems. In similar ways, the supermarket has become a naturalised part of our society. At first they were a novelty; now they are a necessity. In 2009 Tesco's opened 392 stores in the UK – a bad year for retail, with 12,000 independent shops closing down.[15] According to a survey of the New Economics Foundation, 41% of all British towns are 'clone towns' in which over half of all retail outlets are chains.[16] However varied the goods contained within them, these stores confirm the precise opposite of what Zygmunt Bauman claimed when he wrote: 'contrary to the anguished forebodings of the 'mass culture' critics of the 1950s, the market proved to be the arch-enemy of uniformity. The market thrives on variety; so does consumer freedom and with it the security of the system.'[17]

Wal-Mart is a case in point. The first Wal-Mart store opened in Arkansas in 1962. By 1985 it was a powerful regional brand with 882 stores. Today it is the largest company in the world. Measured against GDP, Wal-Mart's annual revenue in 2002 exceeded that of all but 22 nations.[18] The company employs 1.4 million workers in the US alone – this gives it a worker population equivalent to the total population of Auckland, the largest city in New Zealand. Wal-Mart's appeal is easy to explain: its prices are cheap. Charles Fishman explains in the *Wal-Mart Effect* how the company keeps its prices low: by keeping wage costs to a minimum, and by pressuring suppliers to lower 'the bottom line'. One example is the gallon jar of pickles, a year's supply of the US' favourite brand for just $2.97. For fear of losing the contract with Wal-Mart, Vlasic, who supply the pickles, lowered the wholesale price to a level where they could only make one or two cents on each jar. The sheer scale of the Wal-Mart empire gives it this ability to force down supply prices. Every week, Wal-Mart sells 200,000 gallons of Vlasic pickles in their US stores. Not only are suppliers squeezed, so too are competitors. As the company expanded its operations to include clothes, toys, electronic goods and more, the effect on those industries that specialised in such goods was devastating. In 1998 Wal-Mart became the largest retailer of toys, surpassing Toys 'R' Us, sold in 2005 to private equity investors. As with Tesco's and numerous other chains and industries, the more leverage the company has with its suppliers, the more it can expand. Every aspect of the production process is calculated, planned and standardised to minimise costs and maximise opportunities. These processes can be replicated on a global scale: a process that George Ritzer called McDonaldisation. Rationalisation is most visible at the sites of consumption, in our increasingly standardised urban centres, where coffee chains vie for space on every high street, and once-proud cities now compete with out-of-town malls for 'footfall'.

In the 1920s, Hungarian Marxist Georg Lukacs sought to

explain this apparent contradiction between individual choice and cultural homogeneity using the term reification, a capitalist logic which, in Fredric Jameson's words, 'attempts to project a process which separates, compartmentalises, specialises, and disperses: a force which at one and the same time operates uniformly over everything and makes heterogeneity a homogeneous and standardising power.'[19]

'Choice', a signifier of the variety stores contain, is itself reified as the world becomes more – not less – rationalised and standardised, and its products have become more, not less, generic with the same ones filling every store.

It can be difficult to appreciate just how much we are interpellated by brands and how lost we would be without them. This was something I realised when moving to New Zealand in 2009. Many of the brands stocked in UK supermarkets were not available there, with local variations taking the place of UK household favourites. For the first few weeks, shopping was a laborious enterprise of looking carefully at each individual item, figuring out whether it was the equivalent to the one I had in mind. If we had not been socialised into identifying certain styles as suiting us or developing a level of affinity with certain products and brands, shopping would be almost impossible. Chain stores and advertisers play to this need for certainty. However, spurred on by hack postmodern theories, we take consumer choice to mean agency and variety heterogeneity. We flatter ourselves into thinking that our identities are fluid and that advertisers are not influencing our choices. Identities are never tailor-made; they are always (in degrees) off the peg of the production line of a society dominated by exchange-value. Desire inheres in the form that conditions the choices we make.

Experience has folded into hyperreality

'Will there ever be anything so great which is not dehumanised – or a form of happiness which is not tinged with mediocrity',

Lefebvre wondered.[20] For all the uncertainty in the world, what we encounter - even feel - is prepared in advance. Before stepping off the plane the highlights of our destination have already been mapped on iGoogle, the image already fixed in memory. Pleasure is never reached, 'the diner must be satisfied with the menu', said Adorno and Horkheimer.[21] In this disenchanted world we need Disneylands to escape into.

Disney is more than America; it is the world that we see, a world through American eyes. Jean Baudrillard famously called Disneyland a simulacrum of America, a hyperreal more real than reality, an image without depth, without any authentic point of reference: a perfect map of America. The point is similar to the one Debord made about the society of the spectacle, a moment when the commodity has penetrated into every pore of life, from work to leisure and love. Disney is just one of many examples of the commercial Empire, in the case of Disney a 'new means of consumption' including theme parks, shops, satellite television, credit cards, cruise liners and production studios.[22] It is a map of a past that never existed, a fuel-injected experiential present, and an impossible techno-future if the predicted consequences of global warming fully materialise.

Enchantment is itself rationalised in every claim a tourist brochure makes about the adventure, the rush, the excitement and joy – the once-in-a-lifetime experience – of a country, its history and its fantasy rides. New Zealand, a picture of paradise devoid of people and culture in promotional clips, becomes a screen onto which Hollywood fantasies are projected. The most famed of its vistas, the southern fjord Milford Sound, comes with jet boat rides and bungee jumps. A number of tour operators compete for the Lord of the Rings crowd with 'several tours and experiences to cater to your Lord of the Rings needs and hopes'.[23]

Countries become containers in which commodities shuffle, promising re-enchantment by way of a pseudo-Real. And where better to experience this than Auschwitz, a highlight for anyone holidaying in Poland. A virtual tour can be taken before stepping onto the plane, framing a desire to see authentic exhibits and reassuring us that a visit delivers value for money. The user-friendly site boasts two tours called 'Auschwitz I' and now 'Auschwitz II: Birkenau'.[24] Other operators based in nearby Krakow compete for the Schindler's List market, a film that through its seemingly authentic narrative and black and white newsreel style aesthetic has turned ordinary streets unconnected to the actual events into reified sites of tourist pilgrimage.[25] The tour, the site boasts, 'combines insights into Spielberg's film with historical details of the wartime occupation itself.' It also includes a trip to the 'actual site of the Plaszow Concentration Camp... currently on the verge of a major memorial renovation... a visit makes for a deeply moving experience.'[26] Perhaps not as deeply moving as jet boating in Milford Sound.

Deprived of history, consumerism substitutes the once-in-a-lifetime experience, a stage beyond spectacle, a commodity snatched in the bud, a pure present onto which narratives are inserted, the experience never to be forgotten. Susan Stewart, writing on souvenirs, offers an explanation as to their purpose: 'we need and desire souvenirs of events that are reportable, events whose materiality has escaped us, events that thereby exist only through the invention of narrative.'[27] We need 'experiences' and souvenir photos to capture a narrative of the self. With one click of a button we can go on the Auschwitz virtual tour; with another, we can create a 'Museum of Me', an application that Intel have designed for Facebook, enabling people to assemble different bits of their profile and thus 'create and explore a visual archive of your social life'.[28] We search for a token of self that might count for something. Grasping for history, clawing it from memory, we are always travelling, getting nowhere, stumbling, fading, becoming evanescent in search of an inner real. As Baudrillard wrote:

You dream of being yourself when you have nothing better to do. You dream of yourself and gaining recognition when you have lost all singularity. Today we no longer fight for sovereignty or for glory, but for identity. Sovereignty was a mastery; identity is merely a reference.[29]

3.3 Gotta Catch 'em All
A brief history of consumerism

In the period at the dawn of universal suffrage, studies on consumption focused mainly on the bourgeois class: Veblen's *Conspicuous Consumption* and *The Leisure Class,* and Benjamin's *The Arcades Project* are prominent examples. Advertising targeted the elites. With the development of large-scale production, rationalised to maximise efficiency, costs could be brought down and a broader class of consumer catered to. Mass consumption developed alongside mass production and mass democracy. The rising affluence of the post war period, in part due to the concessions the working class had won after sacrifices made on the battlefields, ushered in the 'family wage'. Advertisers began their aggressive targeting of housewives, marketing a series of labour-saving devices and mass entertainment systems for the home. This was the period when Marcuse wrote his seminal work on the one-dimensional society; a period during which youth markets were also aggressively targeted through the Trojan horse of teenage magazines designed to carry marketing messages. The youth rebellions of the 1960s anticipated the end of the 'Golden Age' of the pact between capital and labour – a pact which fully unravelled in the crisis period of the 1970s, by which time consumerism had expanded to all classes and social groups. Even the disgruntled 'subcultures' analysed by the Birmingham School of cultural theorists, Stuart Hall being the most prominent, were being catered to. The defeat of organised labour coincided with the rise of small batch production, deindustrialisation, and the outsourcing of production to low wage economies. The 1980s was a period in which enterprise became the religion of an increasingly individuated but also polarised society. Those seen to have 'made it' became the idols of what was, by the 1990s, named a 'celebrity culture'. Certain individuals became embodiments of lifestyle, fashion, homes and attitudes. Their extravagant lives were reproduced on the high street, first with the likes of Gap, Benetton and Habitat, the latter overtaken by the more rationalised and mass-market IKEA. Postmodern cultural relativism and the premature pronouncement of the end of class politics belied the growing inequalities around the world. Consumers concerned about poverty, AIDS and global warming were a niche market in the 1980s, but by the time Clinton and Blair came to power, companies clamoured for the ethical and ecological clothes which they draped over products fashioned from the earth using cheap labour. The simultaneous rise of the Internet – a technology that appears on the surface to have levelled the playing field by turning everyone into 'producers' – seemed to empower the 'consumers' to take command of their lives in ways inconceivable in the 1960s. Power seemingly transferred to the consumer, the 'prosumer' and the 'consumer citizen'.

The Internet maps already captured desire

The online book retailer Book Depository displays on its homepage a map of the world flashing up purchases at the moment and location they are placed. The world of shopping is displayed before our eyes – an interpassive experience in which the Other enjoys shopping on our behalf. It is a visualisation of Deleuze and Guattari's description of capitalism as an historical epoch in which decoded or excessive flows of desire are endlessly captured and commodified. Capital captures ideas and transforms them into products and services; captures demands for change and transforms them into workplace policy; captures social connections and transforms them into monetised friend networks. Marcuse historicised the Oedipal complex to show that the social demands we submit to are those engineered in the interests of business – he called the associated demand to be economically competitive and calculating the performance principle. Deleuze and Guattari went further by rejecting the idea that desire needs to be repressed at all. Desire, they said, is a productive force on which capital thrives by endlessly capturing it into its circuit.

Desire is channelled through a religion of sorts: the religion of the shopping mall, the interiority of capital, an 'axiomatic' of interiority (commodities and administration) and exteriority (the excessive as yet captured flows of desire), of enclosure and the commons, the commodity and the uncommodified, actual identities and pre-formed becomings. Capitalism is a system of anti-production. It creates upon what it destroys; it captures the excess of desire that threatens it. The deterritorialised flows of the power of labour are captured in the workplace and congealed in the commodity. Oedipus rises. Mommy and Daddy set us to work. Guilty for not having a good time, guilty for not working hard enough: desire is shamed by the Oedipal myth.

The Internet is a perfecting technology of capture, exceeding national boundaries while coding, quantifying and digitising desire. There are multiple pathways available for us to take: we can graffiti the virtual walls without fear of prosecution and paste upon them virtual agitprop posters constructed in Photoshop. The architecture of the Internet and its dominant sites mimics the same economic and power relations protected by states and found on the concrete streets and pathways of New York, London and Tokyo. It virtualises the dialectics of everyday life, the struggle of voices trying to be heard, of ideas, people connecting with one another, forming movements, organising for future political rallies and occupations. As a site of consumption onto which identities are formed the Internet is a technology that allows for a further fetishising of the individual as an autonomous consumer. We travel virtual worlds; we emblazon

Facebook, YouTube or whatever with hastily constructed words and images reinforcing the idea that we are free to make choices in this market economy, unhindered by external forces, a space where every expression is an authentic manifestation of will.

The iGeneration

One of the great misnomers of the Internet age is that people have taken charge of their own creations and thus are freed from alienated labour: the species being returns to its original owner, the 'prosumer'. But the process (and the product) is not so different to a child playing with Lego. The culture industry provides the plastic bricks that we piece together to fashion a Facebook profile, a video clip on YouTube, or a blog of opinions. The iPod operates in a similar way to Facebook, providing the empty form onto which tunes can be uploaded, an infinite variety of options confirming that every individual is different because no iPod shuffle is the same. We insert into these open forms content that the culture industry no longer has to bother assembling, providing the means for us to construct our own narcissistic double. In this sense, capital does not so much *capture* desire as produce the technologies that we can use to capture *ourselves*. We do the job of pseudo-individualising products on behalf of the producer, engaging in a kind of immaterial labour, what Hardt and Negri describe as the production of affect, social connectivity and knowledge, here using materials such as computers and iPods, and sites such as Facebook. Lefebvre wrote that 'bourgeois individualism implies the dreary, ludicrous repetition of individuals who are curiously similar in their way of being themselves and of keeping themselves to themselves, in their speech, their gestures, their everyday habits'.[30] The iGeneration's creations are often every bit as banal, every bit as generic and every bit an instrumental process of turning ideas into commodities.

New media has become the agent of extra-familial socialisation, providing the formatting facility into which subjects process themselves, fishing for and netting an identity with every Facebook thumbs up, the virtual equivalent of the approving reflection in the changing room mirror. Shovelfuls of generic friends flash up on the screen: Todd with his comic moustaches, Miriam who belongs to the group New York Pizza, Travis who likes boats. Into the prescribed template of life we insert nothing of any significance. Our tunes, friends, interests, 'thumbs up' resemble the Panini stickers of football players that boys used to collect and swap for their sticker books.

There is no Immaculate Collection; every box set, friends list and data file has filtered through the commodity. They have been processed and formatted, reproduced, rerecorded and replayed a thousand times over. There is a crisis of virtual overaccumulation. We have collected too much. We have become too many things to too many people with USB storage devices taking up the excess – decentred brains hanging from the key ring, the virtual equivalent of self-storage facilities on the periphery of our cities. We are forced to declutter.

The stars come down to earth
Renata Salecl writes:

> As we work to improve ourselves and our lives, so we need also to create around us the environment best suited to our ideal existence. Since we are increasingly powerless in terms of our ability to change the society we live in, we try to change our immediate environment – our home. The latter may long have been understood as an extension of the self: it is now also an essential part of one's personal development. The house is almost a living thing, something that acquires a certain power over the human subject. Our home is perceived as a prosthesis of ourselves, with the hidden potential to influence our creative self.[31]

What if the objective of decluttering is to achieve nothingness: not so much a refreshing but rather an unconscious purification? Consider programmes advising people how to sell houses. Typically, the seller is told not only to remove clutter but also to paint the walls in neutral colours and, generally, 'keep it blank'. Becoming an individual today means becoming evanescent: one-dimensional becoming undimensional, the subjective equivalent of Coke Zero.

Narcissism, which Lasch described as a grandiose image we have of ourselves, has reached the point where the emptiness of indistinguishable abundance has become the image of grandiosity, the signifier of success in the twilight hour of capitalism, a culture in which everything fertile is finally exhausted.

In *The Man without Qualities* Robert Musil wrote:

> If, in the course of time, commonplace and impersonal ideas are automatically reinforced while unusual ideas fade away, so that almost everyone, with a mechanical certainty, is bound to become increasingly mediocre, this explains why, despite the thousandfold possibilities available to everyone, the average human being is in fact average.[32]

We are switched on to a banal narcissism. The stars come down to earth on reality TV where those similar to (but not quite like) ourselves parade their ordinariness, fascinating and disgusting, too close to reality, too close to what we have become: the uncanny average human being. Freud described the uncanny as the feeling of déjà vu such as we get when encountering a person whose face reminds us of someone we know – a dead relative perhaps – but not quite close enough to be genuinely mistaken for the real thing. The transvestite who is not quite able, despite her efforts, to pass as female has that ghoulish quality about her. We see it in the anamorphic characters of CGI movies targeting children. Increasingly we see it in ourselves, we see the emptiness that alarms and fascinates in equal measure and clamour for ways to be different. We have our opinions, personality and distinctions, we try to exceed a world into which our identities are trapped, but the colours spin into monotone, neutral, insubstantial, blank.

Recalling Nietzsche's *Will to Nothingness*, Žižek claims that the only authentic desire is to desire nothingness itself. But every attempt to create distance from the banality of late capitalism, to cleanse the commodity from our skin through our creations – to will a nameless non-commodity - is simultaneously - if not already - captured into the circuit. Christopher Lasch wrote that 'the banality of pseudo-self awareness becomes so overwhelming that men finally lose the capacity to envision any release at all except in total nothingness, blankness.'[33] Baudrillard made a similar point towards the end of his life in a short book on the disappearance of the subject in which he wrote:

> The subject disappears, gives way to a diffuse, floating, insubstantial subjectivity, an ectoplasm that envelops everything into an immense sounding board for a disembodied, empty consciousness... This is the image of an end-of-the-world subjectivity, a subjectivity for an end of the world from which the subject as such has disappeared, no longer having anything left to grapple with.[34]

The life and death of Jade Goody exemplifies this condition, the ultimate destination of desire. Thinking that Cambridge was in London and Rio de Janeiro a person not a place, Goody's appearance on the reality TV show Big Brother turned her into a household name. Through massive exposure in the media, including sponsorship deals worth millions and eventually her own show, Goody's popularity became a reflection of the aspirations of a culture in which fame in itself had become a mark of success. Her life and death trace the path of never-satisfied *jouissance* driving her to exceed a mere life, to become more than real – more than working class – a hyperreal uncanny celebrity projected into the living room. She entered our world as nobody and became an abject stand-in for the lack in ourselves, only to be exposed and shunned for being racist, and then finally immortalised at age 27 as the tragic victim of cervical cancer and a celebrity-obsessed culture. Her racist outbursts on *Celebrity Big Brother* against her fellow contestant, the Indian actor Shilpa Shetty, prompted media reactions that were more a reaction to the reality that such shows steer *away* from: the caffeine, the sugar, the colour, the harmful substances that speckle a cultural landscape being bleached white with saccharin. It is a culture of death, attesting to the point that – as with Marilyn, Diana and Michael – the only good celebrity is a dead celebrity. Goody came to us lacking: she was neither beautiful nor regal nor talented, and in this respect was the perfect vehicle through which we could interpassively enjoy another person's lack. She lived out *jouissance* on our behalf and showed us what happens when we get what we ask for. She lived the dream and in death became our reality, a subject devoid of politics, devoid of substance. As Adorno put it, the individual still persists amid 'standardised, organised human units... but he is in reality no more than the mere function of his own uniqueness, an exhibition piece, like the foetuses that once drew the wonderment and laughter of children.'[35]

3.4 Gift-wrapped
Liberation is the perfect excuse to be a commodity

We are the consumers and the consumed, producers of bodies and consumers of them, becoming quantifiable entities in CVs, on Facebook and on dating sites. The iron cage has rationalised life and love for the tick box. And we can find love in ten minutes using a '10 minute profile builder', according to the boasts of one dating site. It continues: 'complete these 10 fill-in-the-blank templates, and you'll have a profile that can be copied into any dating site.'[36] With the free 'Dating DNA' app for iPhone, you can turn a personality into a coded sequence of numbers and match them to others to find your perfect lover.[37]

Appearance matters. The idea of the perfect body, complexion, home, husband and children is inculcated in girls from an early age. Much of the advertising in the post-war boom was targeted at housewives who were thought to be the principal consumers of the household. Women were the ones buying the fridges. The one-dimensional 'man' that Marcuse diagnosed was just as likely then, if not more so, to be a woman. But if the movements of the 1960s were to liberate women from the home, that liberation was partial at best. Women were still the cooks, the cleaners, the caregivers and consumers, but now also the wage-labourers with men aggressively recruited from the reserve army of consumers. Today, feminism, according to Nina Power, has bonded with consumerism giving rise to what she appropriately calls a *One Dimensional Woman*. Power writes:

> In [contemporary books on feminism], the political and historical dimensions of feminism are subsumed under the imperative to feel better about oneself, to become a more robust individual...Almost everything turns out to be 'feminist' – shopping, pole-dancing, even eating chocolate... [There are] remarkable similarities between 'liberating' feminism and 'liberating' capitalism, and the way in which the desire for emancipation starts to look something wholly inter-changeable with the desire simply to buy more things.[38]

Feminism has become an exhibition piece; in the 'post-feminist' age the barcode is tattooed on the breasts and vagina. But there were indicators of where feminism might be heading back in the 1950s when Lefebvre wrote that 'promiscuity, infidelity, the absence of jealousy, become signs of freedom, of the new love, of the emancipated 'feminine personality'.'[39] For a short period between then and now, women could define themselves by their politics, rather than their fridges, babies, dietary habits or great nights out. This is not to say that women have come full circle; rather, liberation has become an accoutrement to wear as one would an earring, to be savvy today, sexy tomorrow and the object of the misogynistic pleasures of men joining in the post-feminist celebrations the day after.

Being a woman has become a lifestyle choice, with YouTube make-over videos getting a million hits, and self-help guides such as Jennifer Seeley's *The Transgender Companion (Male to Female)* explaining how to 'act' female:

> Have you always wanted to be a woman, but didn't know how to start? This book will show you! Do you want to know how to look, act, and sound more like a woman, but don't know how? This book will show you! Are you frustrated at not having a single reference on how to transition? This book will give you all the information you need to have a healthy, safe and fun transition to becoming the woman you want to be![40]

As the demand to become a woman increases, the costs go down. Today in Thailand you can become a woman for a little as $6,500 US.[41] Desperate for a Gucci handbag, desperate for a pair of breasts, at these prices more and more people can look on the outside how they feel on the inside.

What is the ideal body? It is a totem, claims Susan Stewart, presenting 'a realm of transcendence and immortality, a realm of the classic.' It is, she says, 'the body-made-object, and thus the body as potential commodity, *taking place* within the abstract and infinite cycle of exchange.'[42] The body has been deprived of its use-value and, in its abstraction, the subject-ness of the self transfers onto a mannequin upon which body parts are added. In America surgeons advertise on television using the slogans of car commercials: 'the best for you, the one you can rely on'. Between 2009 and 2010, over 1.6 million surgical procedures were conducted in the US alone: the majority on women. The top 5 procedures of 2010 were (numbers of procedures in brackets): breast augmentation (318,123); liposuction (289,016); eyelid surgery (152,123); abdominoplasty (144,929); and breast reduction (138,152).[43]

As we adapt ourselves through fashion, dieting, makeovers and surgery, we risk becoming the embodiment of the wrong choice, forever tarnished as a fashion dupe with our 'fish pouts' and pouting profiles. Austerity is a perfect alibi not to make the choice in the first place, but even in times of hardship there are ways and means. Writes Minette Marrin of *The Times*:

> We won't have to try so hard. Less will be calmer; at least we won't have to suffer from choice fatigue. The pursuit of status will seem unkind — unpatriotic almost — as will the relentless pursuit of fashion and style: austerity is a great leveller. Waste not, and in the other sense of the word, want not.[44]

As Adorno and Horkheimer observed, 'In wartime, goods which are unobtainable are still advertised, merely to keep industrial powers in view.'[45] In times of austerity, billboards obscure unemployment and homelessness as we search for more novel ideas on how to be beautiful without it costing the earth. As Papworth, writing in the *Guardian*, observes, 'DIY beauty treatments are flying off the shelves'. Austerity Chic: 'it's about looking good for less'.[46]

Bauman describes a hidden world of 'failed consumers' – the vagabonds – the unwanted or useless excess who cannot afford to shop, who are ignored, isolated and excluded. Their numbers are on the rise. The homelessness charity Crisis reports that there were 10% more people declared homeless in the UK in 2011 than in the previous year; the middle classes are being absorbed into this statistic[47] becoming what Jacques Ranciere calls the (invisible) part with no part. But those on the margins, those with no name, persist as a shadowy presence on our screens and Fairtrade coffee jars. The i of Eros is splashed with the Other's tears. The next chapter is on ethical consumption.

4.0 Conscience

The ethical consumer does not exist

If torture contravenes an established ethical principle then torture for whatever reason cannot be ethically justified. The same goes for ethical consumption. One cannot be an ethical consumer when the form of consumption relies on the exploitation of one class by another. Logos, posters, recycling bins, news items and more, all around us are invitations to consume more ethically and sustainably. And with the knowledge we have about the effects of consumption on people and planet it is hard not to identify with and act upon such invitations. This shift towards a more conscientious form of consumption shows that people are concerned about the issues raised; that, in other words, there is a 'market' for such 'products'. It also shows that capitalism has been able to absorb demands for change into its (ideological) apparatuses of production, distribution and exchange. In doing so the need for urgent and collective action is substituted by a product that we as individuals can purchase without it causing any disruptions to our lives or to the circulation of capital.

This chapter critiques the ideology of ethical consumption: a sign in which capital has invested to denote a conscience, and thereby to disavow the motive of profitability.

4.1 Communicity
The emotive force of communism

Roland Barthes took Saussure's work on linguistic structures and adapted it to analyse visual phenomena. He observed how objects and images operate on different levels of meaning, carrying a range of connotations that advertisers help us translate into a simplified or commonsense language. One example he studied was an advertisement for the pasta brand Panzani. The image was of Panzani products spilling from a netted shopping bag, along with a fresh tomato and mushroom. The predominant colours were green, white and red, the colours of the Italian flag. Barthes said that the image evoked a still-life painting, signalling sophistication, freshness, rural life and Italianicity: a likeness to Italy. Advertisements for Fairtrade products such as coffee and chocolate, as well as the corporate brochures of car manufacturers, oil companies and others promoting their green credentials, function in similar ways. With Fairtrade we typically see a rural scene depicting a developing country, featuring healthy and happy looking dark-skinned people. BP uses images of scientists to promote the idea that profits are being channelled towards developing sustainable technologies. Brands often rely on celebrities to front campaigns such as the Product Red initiative, sponsored by Bill Gates and Bono, to help HIV/AIDS victims in Africa. Standard to all of these images is communicity, an evocation of community, the world together as one united by a transcendent ethical cause. Notions often associated with the left such as equality, fairness and redistribution are being appropriated. Communicity is a kind of ethical uncanny. Business is suspiciously communistic though something is obviously not quite right about their claims of being ethical and ecological.

The signs that construct communicity speak to all of humanity, calling upon the conscientious to act in the cause of social justice and sustainability through their purchases. The sign is potent and proliferate, politically disarming and also profitable, both in terms of generating revenue and improving public images. In 2009, £799m worth of Fairtrade products was sold in the UK. Charitable donations in the UK (represented in US dollars) are around $300 per adult, amounting to $296 billion in 2006 – 75.6% of which came from individual donors. Less tangible is the indirect contribution of consumers who purchase from companies that purport to channel a portion of their profits into charitable schemes: ranging from Starbucks' clean water initiative through to car and oil companies' research and development into sustainable technologies.

The combination of politicians, celebrities, CEOs, popular events such as Comic Relief, corporations, NGOs and so forth involved in ethical campaigns comprise a Culture of Crisis Industry.[1]

The culture industry as apparatus of progressive politics

The Good Guide product rating scheme does the job of working out the ethical and environmental credentials of companies on our behalf. As the site puts it:

> If you are looking to switch to a better product, GoodGuide's summary rating can be used to easily identify the best products in a category. If you are looking for more detail, you can drill down from our summary rating to learn more about a product or company's performance.[2]

By making informed decisions about what to buy, we can go on living with the knowledge of the abjection of those on the margins; those afflicted by poverty and tsunamis. The overall effect of the many companies, politicians, celebrities and emotive campaigns that the public get involved in is to produce a general image of what Žižek has called 'capitalism with a human face' with leading advocates such as Bill Gates being 'liberal communists'. It is a face that stares back at us, imploring us to act, and making us feel guilty if, when confronted with a choice, we refuse to partake in a given action or make that given purchase. The culture of crisis industry evokes and manipulates anxieties about the world, and as with that cream to heal those blemishes, it provides the necessary emollient to smooth them over, an ethical product to heal the wound of exploitation and an eco-friendly product to clean the stain of human life from the environment. In a different register to the culture industry, it helps generalise feelings of responsibility connecting the need to do something about the state of the world with mass market goods and services, profit-making companies and 'not for profit' NGOs. It is the consumer taken by the arm of big business who is made to feel responsible and also empowered when 'doing the right thing'. David Cameron tapped into this sentiment when launching the Big Society agenda. He said:

It's time for something different, something bold - something that doesn't just pour money down the throat of wasteful, top-down government schemes. The Big Society is that something different and bold. It's about saying if we want real change for the long-term, we need people to come together and work together - because we're all in this together....The success of the Big Society will depend on the daily decisions of millions of people - on them giving their time, effort, even money, to causes around them. So government cannot remain neutral on that - it must foster and support a new culture of voluntarism, philanthropy, social action.

In the wake of the devastating earthquake which struck Christchurch in February 2011, New Zealand celebrity Jason Morell-Gunn and his wife Janine launched adoptachristchurch-family.com to raise money for affected families. Those outside the disaster zone were invited to 'adopt' a family as one might adopt an abandoned puppy. The Prime Minister John Key and Crowded House musician Neil Finn added their names to a long list of celebrities sponsoring the charity. The Christchurch appeal is one of many examples of how hardship, famine, torture, HIV/AIDS, environmental destruction, or any image of depri-vation whatsoever, can be turned into objects into which more affluent consumers can pour their compassion and spare change. The causes are never political – except when sympathetic to the dominant powers - the victims always helpless, and the circumstances often framed as contingent, regardless of the fact that disasters often expose how the infrastructure that crumbles to the ground was already dilapidated because of underfunding. 'Give now and lives will be saved', said George W. Bush and Bill Clinton in a global appeal for donations to help victims of the earthquake in Haiti. When those in poverty are represented as victims of earthquakes and famines rather than imperialist crusades or IMF policies, as happened with the Haiti earthquake, the western consumer can become the hero imagining they are a firefighter racing to the scene. Struggle is decentred and the state's role in dealing with emergencies is privatised as the job passes over to individual consumers, NGOs and various for-profit agencies.

The culture of crisis industry spans private enterprise and public institutions, feeding off real-life crises for the purposes of selling products and services – the product of compassionate capitalism, the services of NGOs - buffing up tarnished images with evocations of communicity. The elites become the new champions of the poor, enlightened by realities, enlightening us into the ways of compassion.

From the society of the spectacle to spectacular realism

The Capitocene has given rise to disasters and catastrophes that so far have manifested only as single events such as hurricanes and tsunamis, but these will eventually become a more fluid and everyday occurrence, no longer 'evental' in nature. Naomi Klein cites a number of examples of how companies have benefitted from disasters such as Hurricane Katrina by capitalising on opportunities to rebuild infrastructure and run services that were previously under public control. The culture of crisis industry provides the image to frame such disasters for mass consumption, an image becoming a slide show becoming a movie.

Fantasy is the *mise-en-scene* of desire, providing the form that prepares the predictable shock when the bogeyman suddenly appears in the frame. It is what we expect from the horror genre: making the predictable shock shocking, the kind of shock we received on 9/11 according to Žižek. The disaster movie genre prepares the scene for anything from terrorist attacks to global warming. The 2011 Fukushima earthquake and tsunami is the latest epic following on from films such as *The Day After Tomorrow* and *2012*. SKY Television showcased the tsunami using a movie-style montage, while the *New Zealand Herald* compiled a 'best of' from all the footage people on the scene had taken.[3] A multitude of cine-observers and cine-correspondents volunteer their services where such events take place, providing footage of the spectacular effects of nature, compositions that compete with Hollywood's own phantasmagoria.

Visual media is saturated with images of devastation yet provides no explanation as to the structural factors that lock people into death spirals of hunger, violence, disease and extreme exploitation. Such images are sanitised for our consumption, serving industries whose irresistible marketing ploy is to tell us that, by purchasing their product, the living conditions of those pawned for our compassion will improve. As campaigns to help the poor and dispossessed became TV jamborees, we saw, over the same period, a worsening of conditions for many of those whose faces were perfectly framed to evoke pity. Face to face, Africa to America, the abject could rely only on the grotesque all-you-can-eat buffet of ethical consumption.

'Choice', writes Salecl, 'can open up the possibility of change at the level of society, but only when it is no longer perceived as solely an individual prerogative.'[4] Consumerist ideology is individualistic but it also masquerades as collective and ethical. The company and the consumer become one another's' equivalents, responsible for the plight of others and possessing the means to act on the other's behalf.

4.2 The Fetishisation of Guilt, and its Secret
It is easier to shop than change the world

Just as the worst slave-owners were those who were kind to
their slaves, and so prevented the horror of the system being
realised by those who suffered from it, and understood by
those who contemplated it, so, in the present state of things in
England, the people who do the most harm are the people
who try to do the most good.

Oscar Wilde, *The Soul of Man under Socialism*

A shift has taken place from a superego that commanded us to
enjoy, to one that admonishes us for enjoying too much. The
clearest sign of this is the aforementioned call made by George W.
Bush in 2001 for people to spend their way out of recession and
then, ten years later, Obama's call for a shared sacrifice. The call
to make sacrifices for the good of the economy (while CEOs still
prosper) is daily becoming more strained; the call to make sacrifices on behalf of the poor and the planet remains a powerful one.

The more ethically minded can never do enough to alleviate
the symptoms of poverty and global warming, and so, myself
included, can never get enough of the ethical and ecological
products that satisfy a demand for reductions to poverty and
carbon emissions. The Fairtrade chocolate brand Divine ran a
series of advertisements depicting rural African scenes with
healthy looking black people smiling in the foreground. Images
were accompanied with slogans such as 'Not so guilty pleasure'
and 'Eat Poverty History'. Poverty, rather than chocolate, is the
drawcard. The more of 'it' we eat, the more the poverty of our
politics is put to one side. Our desire to see the end of poverty can
never be satisfied - the image never goes away – and so the
hungrier we are for Fairtrade. Through the mediations of the
culture of crisis industry, capital supplies poverty and chocolate,
cause and solution, fetishising and generalising guilt in the
process. The 'castrated' other – the poor, the dispossessed and so

on - is the carrier of the disease and the container into which, if only temporarily, guilt is atoned for. The other promises guilt-free pleasure to those prepared or able to toss the premium into the proverbial begging bowl provided to the victim during the photo shoot.

While the Internet has made it easier for disparate groups to organise collectively, it also serves to rationalise the commons by digitising death and destruction for virtual consumption. The Cause World iTunes app enables us to earn 'karma points' every time we exchange guilt for one of their causes. It calls itself:

> the first mobile application that lets you do good deeds simply for walking into a store. Sponsors donate real money on your behalf. You choose where it goes. Citibank, Kraft Foods and Procter & Gamble have provided nearly $1,000,000 for you to donate. Simply check in to stores to collect sponsor-backed karmas. Use them to support 18 causes like LiveStrong, American Red Cross, American Forests and more. DONATE FOR FREE. Seriously.[5]

Every mass media campaign for a given cause, whether sponsored by established humanitarian organisations, pop stars and celebrities, politicians, corporations or maverick entrepreneurs, is evidence of the commodification of politics as a substitute for state-based action in some cases, or collective action in others. Individualism prevails.

If global warming did not exist it would have to be invented

There is an urgency to take action when famines hit impoverished regions of the world. The same can be said about the environment. Global warming is the single greatest phenomenon to warrant a general sacrifice, and the most powerful argument for the repression of desire. With the reconfiguration of the superego from one that commands enjoyment to one that commands restraint, global warming provides those who consume the least with a compelling reason to tighten their belts further. Returning to Marcuse's point that the excuse of scarcity weakens as our command over nature increases; the 'feedback' loops of mass consumption on the planet would suggest otherwise. Global warming guarantees that the order of austerity will be endless, that generalised affluence and liberated eros is forever banished to utopia. The culture of crisis industry helps those least affected by the system's enforced austerity to cope psychologically with this, first by shifting the signifier from capitalism as such onto any number of depoliticised terms.

Desire, as the Lacanian scholar Bruce Fink explains, is fundamentally caught up in the 'dialectic movement of one signifier to the next' simply to further its own continuation. The signifier of 'capitalism' as cause of global warming shifts to the signifiers 'green', 'carbon neutral', 'sustainability' and the 'Anthropocene'. Action is oriented to the preservation of nature, while capital inexorably (as is its nature) consumes and commodifies the natural commons. Here the subject can do the ideological work of capital by buying into the myth that progress is possible simply by respecting nature - consuming less, in more discerning ways, and also being less wasteful - and pressuring governments to place limits on carbon emissions. It is as if existing democratic structures and the parties in power are capable of carrying through the sort of reforms needed to prevent the more catastrophic consequences of which scientists almost unanimously warn us. The signifier shifts from the form of production to the content of consumption. Powerless to do anything about global warming at the structural level, we can act as if what we do at the subjective level makes a difference. With our focus on the environment the actual cause of environmental destruction is displaced. The pay off is the palliative. Here from Nature.org:

Walk or bike instead of driving a car. For office meetings, if you can telephone or videoconference, you will save time, money, and carbon emissions. Use compact fluorescent light bulbs. Recycle and use recycled products. Check your automobile monthly to ensure that the tires are fully inflated. Plant native trees. Turn down the heat or air conditioning when you leave the house or go to bed. Buy renewable energy. Shop at a local farmers market and you will find fresh and healthy foods, and help save our climate.

We can check the automobile monthly while keeping the car or get Instant Karma with Air New Zealand, flying around the world and making 'direct contributions' to TrustPower wind farm credits, their carbon offset scheme. The problem is maximal while the solutions are minimal but the marketing ploy is compelling nonetheless. 'Natural capitalism' is filling the gap of the urgent properly political response needed to address the very real problem that we are daily reminded of: it envisages a 'future in which business and environmental interests increasingly overlap, and in which businesses can better satisfy their customer's needs, increase profits, and help solve environmental problems all at the same time'.[6]

From antidote to antidope

In 2011 the *Guardian* website posted what they called an 'interactive labour policy review', enabling people to insert their own ideas on which values Labour should stand for. It read:

> Ed Miliband promised a fresh start for Labour, giving his party 'a blank sheet of paper' on policy. He commissioned policy reviews in 19 areas, and today we're asking you to help Labour fill in that blank sheet. What do you think Labour should stand for?[7]

This follows the myth that our voices count for something: that if we were to suggest, for example, that Labour should stand for social ownership of the 'commanding heights' of the economy, the party would listen and consider it as a policy option. The blank already presupposes that our choices will be 'reasonable' according to what we instinctively know to be Labour's agenda. The same can be said about the ecological strategies we adopt: they are painted onto an already determined blank canvas. 'No Impact Man' is on the eco-vanguard of this post-politics, leading the world through example by demonstrating to the cynic who stupidly thinks she sees through every layer of mystification, or the sceptic on the other side of the fence, that there is a way out of the impasse.

The no impact project is a 'not-for-profit' environmental group with a mission 'to empower citizens to make choices which better their lives and lower their environmental impact through lifestyle change, community action, and participation in environmental politics.' Colin Beavan, the self-defined 'No Impact Man', fronts the enterprise. He wrote a blog, published a book and made a film chronicling 'his family's year-long experiment living a zero-waste lifestyle in New York'.[8] Politically post-political, No Impact Man proposes a fantasy existence in which commodities – whether they be the homes we live in, the materials we use or the tools we buy – really do magically appear on the shelves judging by the fact that the 'impact' of the energy expended in their production, distribution and exchange is never accounted for. It is a middle class fantasy, an empty gesture to all those people unable to afford, indulge in or perhaps have no desire to adopt such a lifestyle or who sensibly reject the logic in the first place.

The Chinese city of Ordos is perhaps the urban utopia of No Impact ideologies. It was built to house over 1 million residents but remains to this day almost empty. There is little in the way of a living community yet thanks to all the money ploughed into the city and a nascent middle class purchasing properties for investment purposes, the model is both economically successful and socially redundant, [9] a model for the rest of the world to emulate.

John Urry proposes a structural variation of the No Impact Project arguing that the 'cluster' of high-carbon systems (located, for example, in the American model of mass consumption) can increasingly be marginalised through progressive policy initiatives that expand the cluster of low-carbon systems developed in the more socially-embedded economies of Europe. Allowing for the moment that a carbon neutral capitalism is possible – and no doubt with considerable effort, technological transfers and so forth, such a thing could be achieved – the political opposition to a root-and-branch transformation would be so formidable that such changes really should be considered utopian. The soft politics of carbon reduction hits against a more organised block of hard rightwing politics. If Obama teaches us one thing, it is that compromise is fatal, and without hard politics on the left, sooner or later the state will have to manage the economy in more aggressive and authoritarian ways to deal with the effects of global warming – that is, if we do not intervene in politically meaningful ways first. This is the topic of the final chapter.

5.0 Commons

Touring without being a tourist

The logic of capital, as Istvan Meszaros says, is deep in every pore of society: it must therefore be eradicated from everywhere. The dilemma we face as consumers is like that of a tourist whose holiday is ruined by the sheer number of other tourists clogging up the streets. How do we improve a situation we ourselves contribute to and cannot extricate ourselves from? How do we get rid of ourselves or withdraw a certain kind of self without negating the vital pleasures that distinguish human life from mere human existence? How do we consume without being 'consumers'?

There are three steps in drug detoxification programmes: evaluation, followed by stabilisation, and finally rehabilitation. The consumer can identify which drugs are circulating in the bloodstream and attempt to stabilise the addiction by limiting the amount of goods she consumes; but she cannot eradicate the toxins, the nasty substance of exploitation, or begin the final stage of rehabilitation until there is change around her. Bringing about such change is the final topic.

5.1 Utopian Realism
The baby that kicks against the womb, hinting at a possible future

To a child returning from a holiday, home seems new, fresh, festive. Yet nothing has changed there since he left. Only because duty has now been forgotten, of which each piece of furniture, window, lamp, was otherwise a reminder, is the house given back this sabbath peace, and for minutes one is at home in a never-returning world of rooms, nooks and corridors in a way that makes the rest of life there a lie. No differently will the world one day appear, almost unchanged,

in its constant feast-day light, when it stands no longer under the law of labour, and when for home-comers duty has the lightness of holiday play.[1]
Theodor Adorno, *Minima Moralia*

'Socialism (the new society, the new life)', Lefebvre wrote, 'can only be defined *concretely* on the level of everyday life, as a system of changes in what can be called lived experience.'[2] There are moments of liberation and joy, utopias in embryo: at a great jazz club, in a thriving co-operative, when engaged in dialogues that inspire thought and action, through the excesses of art, of love. There are embryonic forms of socialism (or communism, or whatever name we want to use) around us and in the many examples scattered throughout history of people coming together in struggles against tyranny and injustice. Perhaps there is hope in the fact that so many people are buying products and engaging in practices that appear to be more ethical and ecological than the alternatives. Change has to happen at the subjective level too, but there are limits both individual and social to how far this can go under current circumstances. Marcuse wrote:

What is now at stake are the needs themselves. At this stage, the question is no longer: how can the individual satisfy his own needs without hurting others, but rather: how can he satisfy his needs without hurting himself, without repro- ducing, through his aspirations and satisfactions, his depen- dence on an exploitative apparatus which, in satisfying his needs, perpetuates his servitude? The advent of a free society would be characterised by the fact that the growth of well- being turns into an essentially new quality of life. This quali- tative change must occur in the needs, in the infrastructure of man (itself a dimension of the infrastructure of society): the new direction, the new institutions and relationships of production, must express the ascent of needs and satisfactions very different from and even antagonistic to those prevalent in the exploitative societies. Such a change would constitute the instinctual basis for freedom which the long history of class society has blocked. Freedom would become the environment of an organism which is no longer capable of adapting to the competitive performances required for well-being under domination, no longer capable of tolerating the aggressiveness, brutality, and ugliness of the established way of life.[3]

When Marcuse talks of a Great Refusal he means a 'rejection of the rules of the game' in the here and now. Refusals of such kind are not always so great though and the results are often patchy at best. Nonetheless we have to begin somewhere, and there are plenty of instances in our lives – at work, in universities and on the streets – where taking industrial action or refusing to comply with managerial diktat, occupying the campus or organising a teach-in, getting involved in a demonstration or blockading Wall Street, can ignite imaginations and stir more people into taking action leading eventually to a more generalised Refusal and revolt.

The 'No Impact' variations and the 'self-sustaining' communities speckling the rural landscapes are a more individualistic and in many ways bourgeois variation of refusal, a distraction from the sort of refusal Marcuse spoke of. Lifestyles and communities that in their practices do not connect with or offer any prospect to the majority of the world's population, especially those living in populous urban environments, are no source of inspiration.

One of the largest and lasting experiments in urban utopias is the autonomous community of Christiania. Set up in the early 1970s by hippies, artists and other renegades of '68, Christiania rose out of an abandoned suburb of Copenhagen and became a 'free' space of individual and collective expression. Impossible to divorce Christiania from the city that surrounded it, high ideals met with the realities of capitalism forcing compromises such as the recent purchase of the land from the state to prevent property developers taking over. Upon visiting Christiania in 2011, the trappings of consumerism were clearly in evidence: computers and mobile phones connected to external networks, cafes with espresso machines, shops with t-shirts and assorted gifts for tourists to purchase. To claim this to be hypocritical is to miss the point though. One cannot do otherwise than engage in contra-dictory practices when there is no practical option to withdraw completely. The refusal can only ever be partial, the subject always has one foot in the door of enterprise and commodity exchange, the excessive i of desire is always prone to capture.

Without giving up on ideas and practices that can improve lives in the here and now – practices that encourage open and critical dialogue - we still need to take action on a broader scale and think bigger than these more localised alternatives to capitalism. We need to think of practical and durable ways to meet the economic needs of the whole of society rather than imagine that we could all somehow survive in island enclaves.

The forces that oppose us are dialectical in nature; industri-alised production, rationalised networks of exchange utilised for one purpose today can be utilised for another purpose tomorrow. By bringing them under common ownership they can be rationalised for our social and environmental needs. A utopian realism (not an original term) is first and foremost a recognition not only that transformation must occur at the very root of the problem but also that the technological forces of production must be fully utilised if everyone's needs are to be met. At stake is the ability to generalise wealth, end austerity and create a material foundation for the liberation of all human faculties, the sensuous life stripped from the body of the subject. Such a vision predicates itself on universal equality, justice and self-determination, and, as this book argues, pleasure too. The possibility of such a future – seemingly impossible under present conditions – will only be apparent from a future standpoint, the future anterior as Žižek explains. It was only when Mubarak was toppled in Egypt that what had, until then, seemed impossible, revealed itself as the hidden dialectic of struggle already alive in that society. There is a tangible hope here and from struggles throughout history, large and small, even those crushed by the forces of reaction. Now is as good a time as any to think upon and enact the impossible.

5.2 Disaster Communism
After the tsunami

The April sun was now well up in the sky, shedding its glorious warming rays on the teeming earth. Life was springing from her fertile womb, buds were bursting into leaf and the fields were quickening with fresh green grass. Everywhere seeds were swelling and lengthening, cracking open the plain in their upward thrust for warmth and light. The sap was rising in abundance with whispering voices, the germs of life were opening with a kiss. On and on, ever more insistently, his comrades were tapping, tapping, as they too were rising through the ground. On this youthful morning, in the fiery rays of the sun, the whole country was alive with this sound. Men were springing up, a black avenging host was slowly germinating in the furrows, thrusting upwards for the harvests of future ages. And very soon their germination would crack the earth asunder.[4]
Emile Zola, *Germinal*

The commodity is the Capitocene's tsunami. The economic crisis – global warming – strews its wreckage, destroying lives, habitats and history, creating a wasteland onto which, as Naomi Klein noted, new seeds of private enterprise are scattered. Saplings crack open the soil, new cities rise, and within them dwell people hardened by the storm, hardened by the realities they are forced to confront. International finance has laid entire societies to waste. Now, like peasants who transcended their own individual limits by combining their labour, people are realising how the power of collective action can sow a different kind of seed – a seed germinating and cracking through the hard soil of capitalism to one day provide a banquet that the entire world can enjoy.

Disaster communism is our shock doctrine. In Argentina, after the economic meltdown of 2001, workers took control of idle factories and brought them back into service: the IMF, the weapon for forcing governments to capitulate to the market, packed their bags and left town. The dialectic is the condition of history – thesis and antithesis, creation and destruction, revolution and reaction. In the 1920s, Berlin – a city ravaged by war and reparations – became a stage inhabited by painters, writers, performers and composers: Georg Grosz, Bertolt Brecht, Marlene Dietrich and Kurt Weill, among others. On the streets of major cities, in communities, workplaces, schools and universities, now under considerable strain, a germ of resistance, a dialogue of ideas, is cracking through the soil – the concrete streets made for cars - with the potential to rewrite history and prevent an ecological holocaust.

Consumer society has developed out of failed revolutions: from the failure of the October Revolution of 1917, with its echoes in the struggles of Weimar Germany in the 1920s, the failure of Mao's cultural revolution in China and the failure of the May 1968 protests in France. It vitalised on the failure of organised labour to win their battle against Reagan or, in Britain, the National Union of Mineworkers against Thatcher with the might of the state behind her. The miners were forced to fight the battle of the decade – for many decades? - in isolation. Their prospects of victory greatly diminished without the broad support of workers and activists outside of the mining industry.

Movements – whether artistic or social, whether made up of paid workers, immigrants, slum dwellers, those behind walls or queuing up at the dole office – must become a singular force if they are to realise their potential to oppose the combined and formidable power of the state and capital, its machinery of destruction, ideologies of fear, cynicism and resentment. Capital flows around the world but it also settles in factories, offices and shopping centres on the streets and at airports where it takes on the appearance of glass, concrete and metal. These are the material sites of production, distribution and exchange where its sinewy veins are exposed. We need to make full use of the resources available to us: human and technical, the intellect and machines. We need organisation. Badiou writes:

> The anonymous action of millions of militants, rebels, fighters, unrepresentable as such, is combined and counted as one in the simple, powerful symbol of the proper name... involved in the operation of the Idea, and... elements of the Idea of communism at its various different stages.[5]

At some point 'Ideas' will need to be translated into actions.

Eros and apocalypse

Marcuse wrote that 'without soil and basis in society, the cultural revolution appears as the abstract negation rather than the historical heir of bourgeois culture.'[6] History teaches us that without transforming the productive base of society, without movements bearing the organisational capacity and strength to smash the bourgeois class and spray weed killer on the seeds it tries to germinate, the cycle of destruction will repeat itself with ever more intensity and with ever greater consequences; humanity will eventually be reduced to a scavenging, brutalised rump.

With no end in sight to the economic crisis and an ecological one promising to become terminal, there is every reason for thinking, as Žižek does, that we are living in the end times. We have reached a phase that is now appropriate to call end-capitalism, a phase of perpetual and amplifying crises that each appear to be 'the final one'. Chris Hedges writes:

> We stand on the verge of one of the bleakest periods in human history, when the bright lights of civilisations will blink out and we will descend for decades, if not centuries, into barbarity. The elites, who successfully convinced us that we no longer possessed the capacity to understand the revealed truths presented before us or to fight back against the chaos caused by economic and environmental catastrophe, will use their resources to create privileged little islands where they will have access to security and goods denied to the rest of us.[7]

Time is not on our side. It is not enough to engage in more localised provocations or take part in occasional protests such as the one in London in 2011 against the austerity measures planned by the government. It is not enough to prepare for another great march in the hope that the government will listen as if our voice actually counts for something to those with the power to decide the fate of the world. Governments and corporations do listen. They have heard the message because they have the surveillance technologies to record it and play it back as evidence if ever they need a justification for imprisoning us. We need permanent protest, such as the Occupy Wall Street movement that threatened to turn into the sort of revolt that inspired revolutions in Tunisia and Egypt. This is just a start, a spark that needs organisation, even leaders, if a global struggle involving students and workers, the disenfranchised and dispossessed, those who suffer gendered violence and the legacies of colonial oppression, is to ignite.

Struggles are often disconnected and unfocused. There are so many causes, so many targets and so many movements; the sum of all these movements is not necessarily greater than their parts. A struggle against the organised power of capital requires an opposing organised movement: not necessarily one coordinated by a party or a small clique of individuals, but one that in its totality combines as a singular and progressive force with the determination to complete the cycle of end-capitalism and end capitalism for the sake of all planetary life, especially humans. We have the capacity to reinvigorate what Marcuse called the great refusal: the refusal to accept the market as the only game in town, the liberal-parliamentary form of democracy as the only legitimate kind of government, the encroachment of the commodity into all aspects of life, humans as irredeemably selfish. In short, we possess the capacity to transcend our condition and create the structural basis from which a different kind of individuality can flourish. Today's Great Refusal is a War on Excess directed not against the self but rather against the apparatus of capital, the apparatus of the performance principle of end-capitalism, the institutions and agencies that steer us ever closer to an endless abyss – justifying endless austerity – the irrationality of the form of consumption and the extinction event of the Capitocene. Unlike Iraq, we see with absolutely clarity that weapons of mass destruction are in the hands of a discernable enemy not an abstraction such as 'terror': their fiefdoms are in every land, and not only in deserts. We need more than the Internet networks, more than the disconnected efforts of individuals, to steer a path clear of this tragedy.

Bauman said that 'with consumption firmly established as the focus, and the playground, for individual freedom, *the future of capitalism looks more secure than ever.*'[8] Capitalism is far from secure and its insecurity stems in part from the fact that the surplus wages paying for mass consumption are every day harder to come by. The point is not to wait for a distant and abstract 'part with no part', the poor of the world, pimped by charity, to rise up. We are already, in one way or another, partially or totally, in and of that situation, the concrete part always hidden, always without a voice or substantive agency. Perhaps there is truth in Mao's statement, recently repeated by Žižek, that 'there is great chaos under heaven – the situation is excellent'. New struggles have emerged from the economic crisis, struggles against austerity, public sector cutbacks - injustices of a system that privileges the financial elites and tries to crush any force that opposes them. These struggles will spread and intensify as catastrophes are rationalised into the apparatus of capital: we need to act now and where the tsunami has already struck, enact the shock doctrine of disaster communism: the people's struggle to create a different kind of society upon an awful situation.

The customer must be satisfied

The living organism, in a situation determined by the play of energy on the surface of the globe, ordinarily receives more energy than is necessary for maintaining life; the excess of energy (wealth) can be used for the growth of a system (e.g., an organism); if the system can no longer grow, or if the excess cannot be completely absorbed in its growth, it must necessarily be lost without profit; it must be spent, willingly or not, gloriously or catastrophically.[9]

Georges Bataille, *The Accursed Share*

It is a dastardly knot that binds the libidinal energy of people with the productive force of capital. The more we pull at one or the other end, the tighter the knot becomes, and the more we are condemned for expending our energy in ways that threaten the material foundation of all existence. But the productive force of desire exceeds its destructive relations and now, more than at any time in its short history, it is apparent that capitalism cannot deliver the goods. Instead of being left wanting, the customers of the world – whether surviving on one or one hundred dollars a day – must be materially satisfied and liberated to pursue gratifyingly humane ends. There is more to lose than our chains, more than our homes, our furnishings, or even our Facebook profiles, our humanity, the civilisations we have created, the planet upon which we depend is at stake. There is a world to win, a world in which the forces of eros and nature are brought into productive harmony.

Austerity or iCommunism, there is no alternative.

Notes to the Text

0.0 Introduction

1   Marcuse, H. (1969). *An Essay on Liberation*. Boston: Beacon Press. p.11.

2   Williams, R. (2005) *Culture and Materialism*. London: Verso. p.187.

3   Washington Post. *Most Americans Don't Blame Obama for Economy, Poll Finds*. Retrieved on 9 November 2010 from http://www.washingtonpost.com/wp-dyn/content/article /2009/03/30/AR2009033003415.html

4   White House. *Remarks by the President in Rio Rancho Town Hall on Credit Card Reform*. Retrieved on 9 November 2010 from http://www.whitehouse.gov/the_press_office/Remar ks-by-the-President-in-Rio-Rancho-Town-Hall-on-Credit-Card-Reform

5   The Guardian. Retrieved on 23 May 2011 from http:// www.guardian.co.uk/politics/2011/mar/25/voters-cuts-coalition-poll

6   Deleuze, G., & Guattari, F. (2003). *Anti*-Oedipus. London: Continuum. p.120.

7   Quoted in Merrifield (2002). p.64.

8   Badiou, A. (2010). *The Communist Hypothesis*. London: Verso. p.47.

9   Badiou, A. (2008). *The Meaning of Sarkozy*. London: Verso. p.98.

Addiction

1   Marx, K. (1990). *Capital: Volume 1*. London: Penguin. p.284.

2   Monster. *What Are My Unique Selling Points?* Retrieved from http://career-advice.monster.co.uk/cvs-applications/cv-advice/what-are-my-unique-selling-points/article.aspx

3   Jameson, F. (2004). 'The Politics of Utopia', New Left Review,

25, Jan–Feb 2004

4   Žižek, S. (2001) *The Fragile Absolute – or Why is the Christian Legacy Worth Fighting For?* London: Verso. p23.

5   Badiou, A. (2007). *The Century.* Cambridge: Polity Press. p.99.

6   Adorno, T., & Horkheimer, M. (1997). *The Dialectic of Enlightenment.* London: Verso. p.154.

7   Adorno, T. (2001). *The Culture Industry.* London: Routledge. p.103.

Excess

1   Bakhtin, M. (1984). *Rabelais and His World.* Bloomington: University of Indiana Press. p.302.

2   Kent, T. (2009). *Rise of the all-you-can-eat restaurant.* Retrieved on 31 January 2011 from http://news.bbc.co.uk/2/hi/8320043.stm

3   The Daily Mail. *What Credit Crunch?* Retrieved on 31 January 2011 from http://www.dailymail.co.uk/news/article-1101 947/What-credit-crunch-Sales-frenzy-grips-Britain-bargain-hunters-queue-2am.html

4   Schneider, K. (2011). *$1bn Streets of Monaco yacht a floating city.* Retrieved on 29 March 2011 from http://www.news.com .au/travel/news/b-streets-of-monaco-yacht-a-floating-city/story-e6frfq80-1225986092068

5   On vacant houses post-2008, see for example: http://finance.yahoo.com/news/Nearly-20-of-Florida-homes-cnnm-2507768369.html [retrieved on 02/06/11].

6   Frank, R. (2007). *The $1 Billion Home?* Retrieved on 30 March 2011 from http://blogs.wsj.com/wealth/2007/07/03/the-1-billion-home

7   Merriam-Webster Dictionary. *Word of the Year 2010.* Retrieved from http://www.merriam-webster.com/info/10words.htm

8   McKie, R. (2011). *Diabetes epidemic affecting 350m – and western fast food is to blame.* Retrieved on 5 July 2011 from http://www.guardian.co.uk/society/2011/jun/25/diabetes-

epidemic-western-fast-food

9   United Nations. *Human Development Report 2007/2008*. Retrieved on 3 June 2011 from http://hdr.undp.org /en/reports/global/hdr2007-2008/

10 The World Bank. Retrieved on 3 June 2011 from http://data.worldbank.org/indicator

11 Schaer, C. (2009). *Tight-belt dressing*. Retrieved on 31 January 2011 from http://www.nzherald.co.nz/lifestyle/news/article. cfm?c_id=6&objectid=10564639

12 Wood, Z. (2010). *Acting rich: recession sees roaring trade in champagne and Louis Vuitton handbags*. Retrieved on 29 March 2011 from http://www.guardian.co.uk/money/2010/apr /13/rich-recession-designer-luxury-brands

13 Field, N. (2011). *Rich back into conspicuous consumption*. Retrieved on 10 April 2011 from http://www.nzherald .co.nz/business/news/article.cfm?c_id=3&objectid=10715523

14 Dorling, (2010). *Injustice: Why Social Inequality Persists*. Bristol: The Policy Press p.161.

15 In Hedges, (2010). *Death of the Liberal Class*. New York: Nation Books. p.197.p.31-2.

16 In Konings, M. (ed.). (2010). *The Great Credit Crash*. London: Verso. p.280.

17 Walshe, S. (2011). *The Right Word: Telling left from right*. Retrieved from http://www.guardian.co.uk/commentisfree /cifamerica/2011/jul/28/fox-news-norway

18 Palma, J. (2009). "The revenge of the market on the rentiers: Why neo-liberal reports of the end of history turned out to be premature." *Cambridge Journal of Economics, 33*(4), 837.

19 Dorling, D. (2010). *Injustice: Why Social Inequality Persists*. Bristol: The Policy Press. p.218.

20 Wall Street Journal. *Should Bush Tell America to go Shopping Again?* Retrieved on 24 June 2011 from http://blogs. wsj.com/economics/2008/10/07/should-bush-tell-america-to-go-shopping-again

21 Turner, G. (2008). *The Credit Crunch: Housing Bubbles, Globalisation and the Worldwide Economic Crisis.* London: Pluto Press.

22 Credit Action 2010

23 Helm, T., & Boffey, D. (2011). *Ministers admit family debt burden is set to soar.* Retrieved on 2 April 2011 from http://www.guardian.co.uk/politics/2011/apr/02/family-debt-burden-government-figures

24 The Guardian. (2010). *Rich list reveals record rise in wealth.* Retrieved on 2 April 2011 from http://www.guardian.co.uk/business/2010/apr/25/rich-list-wealthy-britain

25 Allen, P., & Mead, N. (2011). *Interactive: UK unemployment since 1984.* Retrieved on 2 April 2011 from http://www.guardian.co.uk/business/interactive/2009/jun/22/unemployment-and-employment-statistics-recession

26 For this reason I use the term global warming rather than climate change which is more suggestive of season fluctuation and is therefore less politically salient

27 Harvey, F. (2011). *Worst ever carbon emissions leave climate on the brink.* Retrieved on 4 June 2011 from http://www.guardian.co.uk/environment/2011/may/29/carbon-emissions-nuclearpower

28 Marcuse, H. (2006). *Eros and Civilisation.* London: Routledge. p.92.

29 World Wildlife Fund. (2010). *Living Planet Report.* Retrieved from http://www.worldwildlife.org/sites/living-planet-report/index.html?intcmp=338

30 Slade, G. (2007). *iWaste.* Retrieved on 8 July 2011 from http://motherjones.com/environment/2007/03/iwaste

31 Essick, K. (2011). *Guns, Money and Cellphones.* Retrieved from http://www.globalissues.org/article/442/guns-money-and-cell-phones

32 Marx, K. (1993). *Grundrisse.* London: Pelican. p.99.

33 The Daily Mail. (2011). *Genghis Khan killed so many people that*

forests grew and carbon levels dropped. Retrieved from http://www.dailymail.co.uk/sciencetech/article-1350272/Genghis-Khan-killed-people-forests-grew-carbon-levels-dropped.html

34 Bellamy Foster, J. et al., (2010). p.379.

35 Population Action International. Retrieved from http://www.populationaction.org/Issues/Population_and_Climate_Change/Index.shtml

36 Elliott, L. (2011). *The economy – a Q&A session.* Retrieved from http://www.guardian.co.uk/commentisfree/2011/jul/26/economy-growth-us-debt-eurozone

37 Kay, J. (1998). *Asphalt Nation: How the Automobile Took over America and How We Can Take it Back.* Berkeley: University of California Press.

3.0 Agency

1 Turgenev, I. (1975). *Fathers and Sons.* London: Penguin. p.167.

2 Baudrillard, J. (1998). *The Consumer Society: Myths and Structures.* London: Sage.

3 Hobsbawm, E., & Ranger, T. (2002). *The Invention of Tradition.* Cambridge: Cambridge University Press. p.1.

4 National Retail Federation. Retrieved on 14 June 2011 from http://www.nrf.com/modules.php?name=News&op=viewlive&sp_id=1088

5 National Retail Federation. Retrieved on 14 June 2011 from http://www.nrf.com/modules.php?name=News&op=viewlive&sp_id=661

6 National Retail Federation. Retrieved on 14 June 2011 from http://www.nrf.com/modules.php?name=News&op=viewlive&sp_id=698

7 National Retail Federation. Retrieved on 14 June 2011 from http://www.nrf.com/modules.php?name=News&op=viewlive&sp_id=1056

8 Based on GDP figures from the World Bank. Retrieved on 14

June 2011 from http://siteresources.worldbank.org/DATAS-
TATISTICS/Resources/GDP_PPP.pdf

9   HenNight.co.uk. *Pole Dancing Hen special.* Retrieved on 14
    June 2011 from http://www.hennight.co.uk/package/Pole
    %20Dancing%20Hen%20special

10 StagNight.co.uk. *4x4 Driving.* Retrieved on 14 June 2011 from
    http://www.stagnight.co.uk/activity/4x4%20Driving

11 British Broadcasting Corporation. (2011). *Obama salutes Bin
    Laden raid team in Kentucky.* Retrieved on 14 July 2011 from
    http://www.bbc.co.uk/news/world-us-canada-13313422

12 Al Jazeera. Retrieved from http://english.aljazeera.net/video
    /middleeast/2010/12/201012163026606582.html

13 Commentary in Ranciere, J. (2009). *The Politics of Inaesthetics.*
    London: Continuum. p.78.

14 Marcuse, H. (2002). *One-dimensional Man.* London:
    Routledge. p.193.

15 Glancey, J. (2011). *Time to talk about what we really want from
    our high streets.* Retrieved on 9 June 2011 from
    http://www.guardian.co.uk/commentisfree/2011/jan/10/high
    -streets-specialist-shops/print

16 New Economics. *Reimagining the High Street.* Retrieved on 9
    June 2011 from http://www.neweconomics.org/sites/neweco-
    nomics.org/files/Reimagining_the_high_street_0.pdf

17 Bauman, Z. (1992). *Intimations of Postmodernity.* London:
    Routledge. p.52.

18 Ehrenreich, B. (2011). *Walmart – it's alive!* Retrieved on 9 June
    2011 from http://www.guardian.co.uk/commentisfree/cifam
    erica/2011/apr/01/walmart-alive-us-ruling

19 Jameson, F. (2010). *Valences of the Dialectic.* London: Verso.
    p.204.

20 Lefebvre, H. (2008). *Critique of Everyday Life: Volume 1.*
    London: Verso. p.43.

21 Adorno, T., & Horkheimer, M. (1997). *Dialectic of
    Enlightenment.* London: Verso. p.139.

22 Ritzer, (2005). p.5.
23 Lord of the Rings Tours. Retrieved on 14 June 2011 from http://www.lordoftheringstours.co.nz
24 Auschwitz-Birkenau Memorial and Museum. *Virtual Tour of Auschwitz Sites*. Retrieved on 14 June 2011 from http://en.auschwitz.org.pl/z/index.php?Itemid=8&id=6&option=com_content&task=view
25 See Struk, J. (2004) *Photographing the Holocaust: Interpretations of the Evidence*. New York: I.B. Taurus and Co.
26 Krakow Tours. *Schindler's List Tour*. Retrieved on 14 June 2011 from http://www.krakow-tours.com/tour/Schindlers_List-Krakow
27 Stewart, S. (1993). *On Longing: Narratives of Miniature, the Gigantic, the Souvenir, the Collection*. Durham: Duke University Press. p.135.
28 Intel. *Museum of Me*. Retrieved on 12 July 2011 from http://www.intel.com/museumofme/r/index.htm
29 Baudrillard, J. (2001). *Impossible Exchange*. London: Verso. p.52.
30 Lefebvre, H. (2008). *Critique of Everyday Life: Volume 1*. London: Verso. p.152.
31 Salecl, R. (2010). *Choice*. London: Profile Books. p.34.
32 Musil, R. (1997). *The Man Without Qualities*. London: Picador. p.121.
33 Lasch, C. (1991). *The Culture of Narcissism: American Life in an Age of Diminishing Expectations*. New York: WW Norton & Company. p.98.
34 Baudrillard, J. (2009). *Why Hasn't Everything Already Disappeared*. London: Seagull Books. p.27.
35 Adorno, T. (2000). *Minima Moralia: Reflections on a Damaged Life*. London: Verso. p.135.
36 10 Minute Profile Builder. *Success Stories*. Retrieved on 30 August 2011 from http://www.10minuteprofilebuilder.com/successstories.php

37 Dating DNA, Inc. *iTunes Preview: Dating DNA.* Retrieved on 30 August 2011 from http://itunes.apple.com/us/app/dating-dna-1-dating-app-for/id303973225?mt=8

38 Power, N. (2009). *One Dimensional Woman.* London: Zer0 Books. p.27.

39 Lefebvre, H. (2008). *Critique of Everyday Life: Volume 1.* London: Verso. p.156.

40 Seeley, J. (2007). *The Transgender Companion (Male to Female): The Complete Guide to Becoming a Woman You Want to Be.* CreateSpace Self-Publishing.

41 Bangkok Medical Tours. Retrieved on 30 August 2011 from http://www.bangkokmedicaltours.com/srs_plastic_surgery_thailand.htm

42 Stewart, S. (1993). *On Longing: Narratives of Miniature, the Gigantic, the Souvenir, the Collection.* Durham: Duke University Press. p.133.

43 Plastic Surgery Research. *Cosmetic Plastic Surgery Statistics.* Retrieved on 30 August 2011 from http://www.cosmeticplasticsurgerystatistics.com/statistics.html#2010-FACTS

44 Marrin, M. (2010). *Waste not, want not: here comes the new austerity chic.* Retrieved on 30 August 2011 from http://www.timesonline.co.uk/tol/comment/columnists/minette_marrin/article7127689.ece

45 Adorno, T., & Horkheimer, M. (1997). *Dialectic of Enlightenment.* London: Verso. p.162.

46 Papworth, J. (2010). *'Austerity Chic' is looking good for less.* Retrieved on 30 August 2011 from http://www.guardian.co.uk/money/2010/may/22/austerity-chic-credit-crunch

47 The Guardian. Retrieved in August 2011 from http://www.guardian.co.uk/society/2011/aug/30/homelessness-middle-class-crisis-study

Conscience

1   Cremin, C. (2011). *Capitalism's New Clothes: Enterprise, Ethics and Enjoyment in Times of Crisis*. London: Pluto Press.

2   GoodGuide. Retrieved on 14 September 2011 from http://www.goodguide.com

3   New Zealand Herald. *Video from the quake / tsunami*. Retrieved on 11 May 2011 from http://www.nzherald.co.nz/japan-tsunami/news/article.cfm?c_id=1503051& objectid=10712129

4   Salecl, R. (2010). *Choice*. London: Profile Books. p.148.

5   Retrieved on 18 July 2011 from http://itunes.apple.com/us/app/causeworld/id343905383?mt=8#

6   Hawken, P., Lovins, A., & Hunter Lovins, L. (2008). *Natural Capitalism : Creating the Next Industrial Revolution*. New York: Back Bay Books.

7   Clark, T., Owen, P., & Allen, P. (2011). *Labour policy review – have your say*. Retrieved on 13 July 2011 from http://www.guardian.co.uk/politics/interactive/2011/jun/22/labour-policy-review-interactive

8   No Impact Project. *About Us*. Retrieved on 7 July 2011 from http://noimpactproject.org/explained/

9   Ordos Municipal People's Government. (2009). *Profile of Ordos City*. Retrieved on 7 July 2011 from http://www.ordos.gov.cn/english/eeds2/200908/t20090812_73327.html

Commons

1   Adorno, T. (2000). *Minima Moralia: Reflections on a Damaged Life*. London: Verso. p.112.

2   Lefebvre, H. (2008). *Critique of Everyday Life: Volume 1*. London: Verso. p.49.

3   Marcuse, H. (1969). *An Essay on Liberation*. Boston: Beacon Press. p.4.

4   Zola, E. (1954). *Germinal*. London: Penguin. p.498-9.

5   Badiou, A. (2010). *The Communist Hypothesis*. London: Verso.

p.250.

6   Marcuse, H. (1972). *Counter-revolution and Revolt*. Boston: Beacon Press. p.93.

7   Hedges, C. (2010). *Death of the Liberal Class*. New York: Nation Books. p.197.

8   Bauman, Z. (1992) *Intimations of Postmodernity*, London: Routledge. P.51.

9   Bataille, G. (1998). *The Accursed Share*. New York: Zone Books. p.21.

A dialogue continues on iCommunism 2.0
www.icommunism.org

Contemporary culture has eliminated both the concept of the
public and the figure of the intellectual. Former public spaces –
both physical and cultural – are now either derelict or colonized
by advertising. A cretinous anti-intellectualism presides,
cheerled by expensively educated hacks in the pay of
multinational corporations who reassure their bored readers
that there is no need to rouse themselves from their interpassive
stupor. The informal censorship internalized and propagated by
the cultural workers of late capitalism generates a banal
conformity that the propaganda chiefs of Stalinism could only
ever have dreamt of imposing. Zer0 Books knows that another
kind of discourse – intellectual without being academic, popular
without being populist – is not only possible: it is already
flourishing, in the regions beyond the striplit malls of so-called
mass media and the neurotically bureaucratic halls of the
academy. Zer0 is committed to the idea of publishing as a
making public of the intellectual. It is convinced that in
the unthinking, blandly consensual culture in which we live,
critical and engaged theoretical reflection is more important
than ever before.